The Good Path

Thomas Peacock   Marlene Wisuri

Ojibwe
learning and
activity book
for kids

Minnesota Historical Society Press

Publication of the first Afton Press edition of this book was made possible with generous financial support from the Target Foundation, Lucy C. MacMillan Stitzer, and Mary A. Anderson in memory of William R. Anderson.

Publication of the Minnesota Historical Society Press edition of this book was made possible in part with generous grants from the June D. Holmquist Publications and Research Fund and the George A. MacPherson Fund.

First published 2002 by Afton Historical Society Press

www.mhspress.org

The Minnesota Historical Society Press is a member of the Association of American University Presses.

Manufactured in China by Pettit Network, Inc.

10 9 8 7 6 5 4

∞ The paper used in this publication meets the minimum requirements of the American National Standard for Information Sciences—Permanence for Printed Library Materials, ANSI Z39.48-1984.

Cover: The Bear Clan by Ojibwe artist Joe Geshick. The old woman inside the sweat lodge represents the honoring of the four stages of life: infancy, youth, adulthood, and old age.

International Standard Book Number
ISBN-13: 978-0-87351-783-6
ISBN-10: 0-87351-783-0

Library of Congress Cataloging-in-Publication Data

Peacock, Thomas D.
    The good path / Thomas Peacock and Marlene Wisuri.
        p. cm.
    "First published 2002 by Afton Historical Society Press."
    ISBN-13: 978-0-87351-783-6 (pbk. : alk. paper)
    ISBN-10: 0-87351-783-0 (pbk. : alk. paper)
    1. Ojibwa mythology—Juvenile literature. 2. Ojibwa Indians—Religion—Juvenile literature. 3. Ojibwa Indians—Social life and customs—Juvenile literature. I. Wisuri, Marlene, 1940– II. Title.
    E99.C6P398 2009
    299.7'8333—dc22
                                                            2009033434

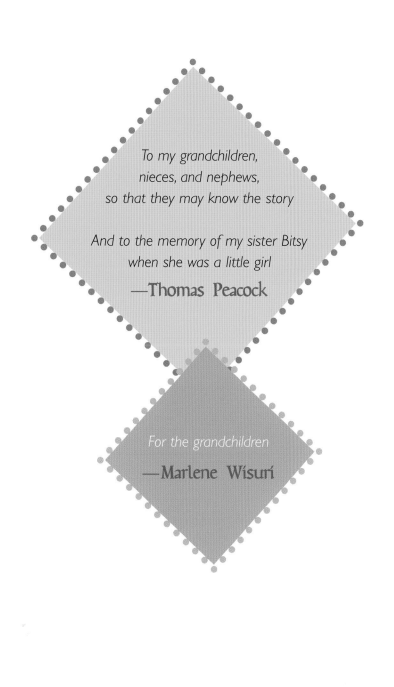

To my grandchildren,
nieces, and nephews,
so that they may know the story

And to the memory of my sister Bitsy
when she was a little girl

—Thomas Peacock

For the grandchildren

—Marlene Wisuri

CONTENTS

INTRODUCTION

This is the story of our people, the Ojibwe—native people who live in southern Canada, Minnesota, Michigan, Wisconsin, North Dakota, and parts of Montana. The Ojibwe story combines history with cultural stories and introduces you to the Good Path—the values that form Ojibwe philosophy (ways of thinking, being, and living).

The Ojibwe story spans all time, from creation to the present day. As you read *The Good Path,* you will learn the Ojibwe creation story and hear about the destruction and re-creation of the Earth following a great flood. You will meet the Lenni Lenape, the ancestors of many native tribes, including the Ojibwe. You will see how women are important to Ojibwe people. You will understand how prophecies (predictions about the future) led the Ojibwe on a westward migration from the Atlantic coast to Madeline Island in northern Wisconsin. You will see

how Ojibwe life changed after the coming of Europeans. And you will learn about the hopeful future that awaits all people, including the Ojibwe.

In traditional times, storytelling was the primary way that Ojibwe elders and other teachers passed the values of the Good Path from generation to generation. The nine values of the Good Path ask people to honor the Creator, elders, women, and plant and animal beings. They ask people to be peaceful, kind, moderate, and courageous. And they ask people to keep their promises. The Ojibwe believe that to live these values (to act on them) every day is to have attained wisdom.

Because the stories were not written word-for-word, Ojibwe storytellers relied on memory and often added their own interpretations. That is the nature of the oral tradition (the telling of stories and teachings using spoken stories), and that is why the stories in this book use different teachings and writings of several Ojibwe historians.

In the Ojibwe world-view, common threads exist among cultural stories, beliefs, and history. All represent fractions of the truth, and that is why the Ojibwe do not refer to these cultural stories or beliefs as "legends" or "myths." We hope you will do the same. Because *The Good Path* is written from an Ojibwe world-view, certain parts that deal with troubling historical events (such as the removal of Indian children from their families to place them in boarding schools) may make some nonnative people uncomfortable. We believe the healthiest way to deal with these issues is to confront them, understand them, and then move on, without blame or guilt.

You may have heard the Ojibwe referred to as the Anishinaabe, Chippewa, or Ojibway people, but we refer to ourselves more often as "Ojibwe" when identifying ourselves as a tribe. There are also different ways of spelling in Ojibwe, including the double-vowel system used in this book. Practice using the Ojibwe words used throughout *The Good Path,* which introduce you to our language. Don't worry about mispronouncing the words!

In many ways, the values of the Good Path are universal. Knowing these values is simple. Following them is difficult. We hope the special kids' activities listed after each chapter will help you to remember the Good Path and to follow it in your own life.

 ◆ Thomas Peacock
 ◆ Marlene Wisuri

Today I ran along the road to Little Sand Bay (Red Cliff, Wisconsin).

A golden eagle circled just above me, and soon another one joined it.

I was at once overcome with love for my Creator, who had given me

that moment and has given me a life in the circle of love of others.

—Thomas Peacock

CHAPTER ONE

The Creator's Vision

This is the Ojibwe story about the creation of the universe, the stars and planets, the Earth, and humankind. It is a beautiful and ancient story, many thousands of years old, and was told to Ojibwe children long before the coming of Europeans to North America. In the telling of the story, children learned the value of *honoring the Creator.*

THE CREATOR'S DREAM

All stories have a beginning. In the beginning, there was nothing in the universe but the Creator, *Gitchi Manitou* (Great Spirit), the Great Mystery. The Creator is all-powerful and all-knowing. The Creator is everywhere and in all things.

In the beginning, the universe was dark. And when the Creator would send out a voice, it would return without being heard by another being. The Creator was lonely. Then the Creator had a dream, a vision, and it was a beautiful dream. In it the Creator saw all the things that would be created.

The Creator's dream was of a universe full of galaxies, stars, moons, and planets. Of the sun, moon, and Earth. The Creator saw Earth with its oceans, forests, deserts, mountains, plains, valleys, lakes, and islands. And the Creator saw all the kinds of flowers, trees, grasses, and other plants that were to live on Earth.

The Creator saw all the beings of Earth: the four-leggeds, birds, fish, and creatures that crawl. The Creator saw how all the living things of Earth were born, grew, and died. And the Creator also saw how new life was born when living things died so that the circle of life would continue.

13

The Creator had a dream, and it was a most beautiful dream. The Creator saw a universe full of galaxies, stars, moons, and planets.

The Creator heard all the sounds of Earth: the crashing of waves, the rumble of volcanoes, the thunder, and the wind. The Creator heard the sounds of all the animals for the first time: the roar of lions, the chatter of monkeys, and the beautiful voices of songbirds.

The Creator's arm reached down and felt the wind and rain. And the Creator felt the emotions of the creatures on Earth for the first time as well: love, hate, jealousy, wonder, contentment, sadness, happiness, fear, and courage.

The Creator thought about the dream and tried to understand what it all meant:

In his [his/her] wisdom Kitche Manitou understood that his [his/her] vision had to be fulfilled. Kitche Manitou was to bring into being and existence what he [he/she] had seen, heard and felt.[1]

THE CREATOR FULFILLS ITS VISION

First the Creator made all the kinds of wind, water, rocks, and fire. And the Creator breathed onto them and gave them life. Each of these substances was given some of the Creator's power, and that power

The Creator gave water gentleness as well as the ability to crash in large waves.

Flowers and bees both need each other to live. Flowers need the bees to pollinate and bees use flower nectar for food.

became its soul. Wind was given gentleness as well as howling. Water was given calmness and the ability to crash in large waves. Fire was given warmth and the ability to destroy. Rocks were made, from the smallest grains of sand to the tallest mountains.

From each of these four substances, the Creator made all the galaxies, stars, planets, and moons of the universe. Then the Creator made our sun, moon, neighboring planets, and, finally, the Earth. Our beautiful Earth was filled with oceans, lakes, rivers, and streams. And the Creator made all the kinds of land: mountains, plains, forests, and deserts. All of the things of the Earth were given a reason for their existence, a purpose.

Then the Creator made all the plants of the Earth, and there were four kinds: vegetables, trees, grasses, and flowers. Each was given life and made to partake in the great circle of life that is birth, growth, death, and rebirth. The Creator put everything in the places on Earth where they would be the most beautiful and useful to each other.

Then the Creator made all the animal beings: birds of all kinds, whales and fish, reptiles, amphibians, and mammals. For the first time, animals flew, walked, and swam on Earth. Deer ate the grasses and flowers from meadows. Fish jumped. Eagles and hawks circled high above Earth. Each of Earth's creatures was given some of the Creator's power and some of the Creator's nature.

Last, humankind was created in all shapes, sizes, colors, languages, and ways of living. Humans were given several gifts not given to the plants or animals. The first was the ability to dream. When humans were given the gift of dreaming, we also were given the ability to create and invent things, and to find ways to make our dreams come true. Then we were given a special gift: Each and every one of us was given some of the Mystery, some of the Creator. The parts of each of us that come directly from the Creator are the values of the Good Path. Each of us was born with these values already in our hearts. These values include:

- Honor the Creator
- Honor elders
- Honor women
- Honor our elder brothers
  (the plant and animal beings)
- Be peaceful
- Be kind to everyone, even those
  with whom we disagree
- Be moderate in our thoughts, words, and deeds
- Be courageous
- Keep our promises

The Ojibwe call living these ways the Good Path.

Then the Creator made the laws to govern all creation

so there would be harmony among all things, creatures, and humankind. And each law was formed into a great circle. The Creator made the galaxies rotate in circles and clustered them so they circle around each other. Stars circle the galaxies, planets circle the stars, and

Deer ate the grasses and flowers.

Humankind marvels at all of creation.

moons circle the planets. The wind circles the Earth. Fire gives light to create life and takes life as well. Rocks become sand or melt in heat, and then mold back into rock, only to become sand again. All creatures experience birth, growth, death, and rebirth. This is the great circle of things.

The Creator's vision came true.

THE FLOOD

For a long time, there was harmony on the Earth. People got along and helped each other. Children respected their parents. Marriages were strong between husbands and wives. Elders were respected. The people cared for the Earth and all the animals and plant beings. Lakes and rivers were clear and unpolluted. In turn, the Earth gave its bounty back to humankind. People always had enough food. Animals offered themselves freely to humans as food, and the Earth grew all the vegetables the people needed.

Then something happened. People began arguing. Families were torn apart in these arguments. Neighbors

The first gift to humankind was the ability to dream. By enabling us to dream, the Creator gave us the ability to create and invent things.

fought against neighbors, villages against villages, and nations against nations. People began killing animals for no purpose other than to kill. Crops failed. Drought and storms came. The Creator was sad at seeing these things and waited a long time for them to change for the better, but things only got worse.

The Creator decided the only way to rid the Earth of all the evil was to purify it, and decided to do it with a great flood. It began to rain and didn't end. Villages were flooded. The people went into the safety of the hills, but soon the water rose above the hills. The people went into the safety of the mountains, but soon the water rose above the mountains. The animals also sought safety, but they had to swim to stay alive. Even the birds had no place to land.

Loon dived in and was gone a long time.

It was at this point that *Waynabozho* came along. Waynabozho was half-human, half-spirit. He would become a great teacher of the Ojibwe people. He too was trying to save himself, and he climbed onto a giant log to keep from drowning. Animals of all kinds joined him on the log: cranes, raccoons, rabbits, foxes, and badgers. Birds of all kinds circled above the log: gulls, hawks, eagles, robins, and jays. The swimming creatures came to the log as well: beavers, muskrats, fishes, and turtles. When the swimming creatures became tired, they would rest on the log and then re-enter the water. Birds would do the same, taking turns resting on the log and then flying until it was their turn to rest again. In this way, the animals saved themselves. Finally, Waynabozho told the animals that he would try to swim to the bottom of the water and find some land:

I am going to do something, he said. I am going to swim to the bottom of this water and grab a handful of Earth. With this small bit of Earth, I believe we can create a new land for us to live on with the help of the Four Winds and Gitchi Manitou.[2]

So Waynabozho dived in and disappeared into the water. He was gone a long time and the animals feared he had drowned. Finally, he came to the surface. At first he was so out of breath he couldn't speak. When he could speak, he told the animals he did not have the strength to reach the bottom. The water was too deep. The animals sat in silence for a long time, wondering what they would do.

"I'll try to get some earth," said Loon. It dived in and disappeared into the water. It was gone a long time. When it finally surfaced, Loon had no earth.

"There is no bottom," it said.

Next to try were Helldiver (a grebe, a diving bird) and then Mink, Otter, and Turtle. All failed. Finally, Muskrat said it would try. All the animals laughed. If they couldn't make it, how could lowly Muskrat do it? But down into the water went Muskrat, and it was gone for a very long time. Finally, Muskrat's body floated to the surface. Everywhere, a mourning song was heard. When Waynabozho held the body of Muskrat in his hand, he noticed that Muskrat tightly grasped a small ball of earth. Muskrat had sacrificed himself so they could be saved.

HONOR THE CREATOR

Waynabozho took the ball of earth from Muskrat's paw. Then Turtle swam forward and offered its shell to hold the earth. And the Four Winds blew in all directions to scatter the earth. The earth grew into a large island, and the animals and people had a new Earth upon which to start over. A great celebration took place, and all gave thanks and honored the Creator.

And that is why the Ojibwe call this special place on which we live Turtle Island.

We call this special place on which we live Turtle Island.

ACTIVITIES

TEST YOUR MEMORY

- The Ojibwe believe in a higher power, the Creator. What was the Creator's dream?
  According to the story, how did the Creator make the dream real?

- The Ojibwe believe that all humans are born with the values of the Good Path in them.
  What are these values, and what do they mean to you?
  Can you give examples?
  How are these values the same or different from the values some people believe in today?

- The Ojibwe believe a flood covered the earth. Why was there a flood?
  What happened in the flood?
  How did animals and people survive?

GOOD PATH PROJECTS

- Create drawings of the universe with stars, galaxies, planets, and moons.
  Create drawings of the earth and its physical makeup (mountains and oceans, for example),
  animals, plants, or different cultures of people.

- Illustrate some or all of the Ojibwe creation story using your own art.
  Write important parts of the story at the bottom of your picture.

- Use books or the computer to learn about creation stories or flood stories from
  different cultures.
  How are they similar?
  How are they different?

I remember my grandfather. His house once cleaved a stand of lilacs and willow at the end of an old road. He lived in Fond du Lac Reservation (Minnesota) near a hill that overlooks the river flowing through Nahgachiwanong (place where the water stops). He would tell stories in the dark quiet of winter evenings. He has been gone for many years, but I carry his memory when I walk the hills and fields of that sacred land. In the warm rain that lights upon summer grasses, in the singing of trees and wind, and in the hushed quiet after heavy snow, his spirit runs through the land, in the deep still of that place.

—Thomas Peacock

CHAPTER TWO

The Grandfathers

Long before the Ojibwe, there were the Lenni Lenape. This is their story.

The Lenni Lenape are the ancient ancestors of the Ojibwe. Known by the Ojibwe as the Ancient Ones, or Grandfathers, the Lenni Lenape are the people from whom many tribal nations originated. Their story connects the Ojibwe as relatives to many other tribes. And because the Ancient Ones are our traditional Grandfathers, the Ojibwe honor them as we *honor all elders.*

THE LENNI LENAPE

In the oral (spoken) history of the Ojibwe, there were stories about a time when our people lived in the west. It was said that they had lived in the east (on the Atlantic Ocean) for so long that many forgot their *true* homeland was in the west. The written history kept by our Lenape ancestors shows that to be true.

The Lenni Lenape kept a written record of their history going back more than seventeen hundred years, perhaps to A.D. 300. This history, called the *Wallam Olum,* is the oldest written record of native people in North America. It is written in song and recorded on wood and bark tablets. The Wallam Olum tells of the Lenape's great migration from the west to the east, where they eventually settled in the beautiful Delaware River valley along the Atlantic Ocean.

Who were the Lenni Lenape? They were a *nation,* just as the United States or Canada or Afghanistan is a nation, each with its own territory and government. There were many *tribes* (social groups of many families, clans, and generations) of the Lenape. And each tribe had different *clans* (groups of people whose households claim descent from a common ancestor).

Long before Europeans migrated to North America, the eastern woodlands were the homeland of Lenape-speaking people. The Lenape-speaking tribes share similar cultures and languages. Native speakers of Ojibwe, for instance, can often understand and converse with their Lenape relatives, including the Ottawa, Potowatami, and Cree. All Lenape-speaking people share a common origin in the Lenni Lenape, the Grandfathers.

Ojibwe elders have told stories to the young for thousands of years.

The Lenape were forest people who lived in small, seasonal villages. Their government was a democracy with councils headed by leaders called *sachems,* whose only authority came from their ability to persuade others. Families were related through their clans—the Turtle, Turkey, or Wolf clan. Marriage within clans was prohibited. Clan membership was important, even more important than being a member of the tribe. Elders were given great respect and *honor* in Lenape culture.

Village life revolved around the seasons. In the spring the Lenni Lenape would gather near the water. There they would harvest spawning fish, hunt animals that gathered nearby, and pick berries. In the summer the people would disperse (spread out). Some would go to the seashore to gather shellfish. They also used the shells to make *wampum* belts. Wampum was used like money in trading. It was also strung in patterns to tell stories and relay messages from village to village, as well as to communicate with other Lenape tribes. Most Lenape, however, moved inland during summer to work gardens they planted in the river bottoms. Corn, beans, squash, and tobacco were grown. Autumn was the time for group hunts, when large game was harvested. In the winter, the Lenape would sit comfortably in their wigwams (dwellings), telling stories and making items for everyday use and for trade.

THE MEANING OF THE WALLAM OLUM

The Wallam Olum is an epic song containing only 687 words and using 183 symbols. Each word is filled with meaning and contains a whole story or series of stories. When the song was sung long ago, the words must have reminded the singers of other, more complete accounts of happenings and events. Nearly one hundred generations of history were recorded in the song. Linda Poolaw, Grand Chief of the Delaware Nation Grand Council, said of the Wallam Olum:

It is an old song, by an ancient people. I believe it was sung by the Grandfathers. I believe it was sung many, many times for many, many centuries. I believe it was sung by my ancestors, as they traveled thousands of miles in search of that place where the Sun wakes up. I pray that this song of the Lenape will be heard. Listen.[3]

The Lenape kept other important written records.

Sacred songs were put on prayer sticks, or song sticks, which were wooden tablets carved with the written language. Family histories were kept, which described the character of individuals. The language was written on rocks, stones, bark, and wood to record events, achievements, and information. The Ojibwe kept similar written records.

The story told in the Wallam Olum begins at the time of creation. The world was covered with water. From out of the deep came a mist and within it moved the

The Lenape used shells to make wampum belts. Wampum was also used like money for trading, and strung in patterns to tell stories and to relay messages from village to village.

The Lenape kept written records on rocks, stones, bark, and wood to record events, achievements, and information. The Ojibwe kept similar records.

Creator, who is eternal and omnipresent (is every-where and in everything all of the time, including the past, present, and future). The Creator made the sky, heavens, stars, and planets and made all things move in harmony. Then the mist and waters that covered the Earth parted and the land emerged.

The Creator then made the spirits (*manitou*) and the souls of all living things. Then Ancestral Man and the Mother of Life (the first of all mothers) were created, and she gave the Earth all the creatures of the air, land, and water.

In the beginning, life was good. The spirits took good care of the people, bringing men and women together and providing food for them. Then an evil spirit in the form of a serpent taught men to kill each other using sorcery. Storms, sickness, and death came upon the world for the first time.

THE FLOOD

Among the Lenape-speaking people, there are many versions of the flood story. Which one is the truth? Probably all of them woven together form the whole story. We will never know. Here is the story told in the Wallam Olum.

The evil serpent and humans fought for a long time. Then the serpent caused a great flood in an attempt to wipe out all people. An island, a giant turtle, was the only thing that remained above the floodwaters. On the back of the turtle was *Nanabush* (Ojibwe call him Waynabozho or *Nanabozho*). Nanabush helped the people and other living things onto the back of the turtle. The Spirit Daughter helped him. The survivors became known as the Turtle people. These people sent a diving creature down into the water to recover a piece of earth. The Earth was restored.

THE MIGRATION BEGINS

The Turtle people lived in caves, and the land was very cold with snow, storms, and ice:

Their home was icy.
Their home was snowy.
Their home was windy.
Their home was freezing.[4]

This may have been during the end of the last Ice Age, more than eight thousand years ago. But to the north there were large herds of animals to hunt, so the people moved. Some readers of the Wallam Olum believe this part of the song proves that the Lenni Lenape came from Asia and that the land being described is Siberia. Many native people, however, believe the Lenape and their descendants originated here in North America.

The Lenape had a great war with their enemies, the Snakes, and defeated them. The Snakes fled across a channel in the ocean into the land of *Akomen* (meaning "Snake Island," "the Wilderness," or "the Land Beyond." The Wolf and White Eagle clans of the Lenape settled along the ocean. They rowed across an ocean channel to Akomen and found a land of bounty.

THE NORTHWEST COAST

The Lenape migration story recalls a time when they may have lived on the northwest coast of what is now the United States. For a while their lives must have been good compared with earlier times. Fishing, especially the annual migration of salmon, would have provided them with an easy source of food. Soon, however, came a long succession of leaders who led them into war. None of the leaders is mentioned by name, in keeping with the Lenape belief that bad people should be forgotten. Two northern-California Lenape-speaking tribes, the Yurok and the Wiyot, may have stayed in the west while the others migrated toward the east.

A significant event occurred during this time. *Olumapi* (History Man) invented the written language, which the Lenape would use to chronicle their journey.

Long ago our ancestors lived in a region that was cold with snow, storms, and ice.

THE GREAT PLATEAU

The migration took the Lenape into the Great Plateau, east of the Cascade Mountains. Here their way of life changed again. They raised crops and gathered the wild edible (eatable) roots, grains, and fruits that grew plentifully in their new homeland. In the spring they harvested the migrating salmon that ran thick in the rivers. Then a great drought occurred. Plants withered and died. Rivers ran dry:

> There was no rain,
> No food to gather;
> Eastward they went
> To where there was water.[5]

THE HIGH PLAINS

Many Lenape perished during the drought. The survivors continued their migration to the east. They traveled through the high mountain passes of the Rocky Mountains and into the High Plains. Here they moved along the river valleys of what some historians believe are the Saskatchewan River to the north and the Missouri-

Yellowstone Rivers to the southeast. The Cree, Algonkins, and Montagnais, all Lenape-speaking people, may have separated from the main group of Lenape during this part of the journey.

The Lenape may have settled for a time along the Yellowstone River near what are now Wyoming and Montana. Lenape-speaking tribes, including the Blackfoot, Cree, Arapaho, and Cheyenne, still live in that area. At each stop along their eastward journey some Lenape would stay, while the main group would continue on their way.

ENCOUNTER WITH THE MOUNDBUILDERS

The Lenape's eastward journey continued toward the rising sun, the source of life. When they arrived near the Mississippi River, they came upon the earthen lodges of the Talegas, the great Moundbuilders, and their walled city of Cahokia. From the western side of the Mississippi River, the Lenape sent a message to the Talegas, asking permission to settle in the area. The request was denied, but they were told they could travel through the area unharmed. But when the Talegas

The migration continued through the high mountain passes of the Rocky Mountains into the High Plains.

saw the great numbers of Lenape crossing the river, they became frightened and attacked. Many Lenape lost their lives. They fought back and were soon joined by new allies, the Iroquois. Victory came after hard-fought battles.

The Wallam Olum records that the Lenape had four leaders during the great struggle. After the war the allies divided the land. The Iroquois took possession of the area around the Great Lakes and the Lenape occupied the Ohio Valley.

THE OHIO VALLEY

The Lenape called their new home Talega, in memory of their defeated enemies. They flourished by growing large gardens of squash, beans, and corn. Their villages grew in numbers, and they became well-respected traders known for hundreds of miles around. Then came a time of drought. Crops failed and people went hungry.

Some Lenape left the Ohio Valley and eventually formed their own tribal nations. The Nanticokes traveled through the Cumberland Gap into Virginia and eventually settled in the tidal basin of Maryland. The Shawnee moved deep into the South. Still the Lenape kept on their journey. Some went north into the Great Lakes region, where Lenape-speaking tribes still live, including the Fox, Sauk, Ottawa, Potowatomi, Menominee, and Ojibwe.

EASTWARD TOWARD THE DAWN

The Lenape journey from the Ohio Valley to the Atlantic Ocean took forty years. They traveled through the

The Lenape traveled through the Allegheny Mountains, finding at long last their home on the Delaware River.

valleys of the Allegheny Mountains, finding at long last their home on the Lenape River (now the Delaware River). Here they stood on the shore of the Atlantic Ocean, where the sun first rises over the continent. To celebrate the event, they began a special calendar belt of wampum, with a bead added every year. When the beads were counted many years later, it showed the Lenape had arrived on the East Coast in 1396. From there, some headed toward what is now New England, where they formed other tribal nations. Among them are the Lenape-speaking tribes of the Nipmuc, Narraganset, Montauk, Wampanoag, Pequot, Nantascot, Passamaquaddy, and Penobscot.

THE ENCOUNTER

The Lenni Lenape lived along the Lenape River for nearly 250 years before they encountered the white race. The arrival of Europeans along the eastern seaboard would forever change life for the Lenape and all other native people.

In 1610, Captain Samuel Argall of England explored near the Lenape River. He renamed it the Delaware

River after Sir Thomas West, who was Lord de la Warr and governor of the colony of Virginia. From that time forward, the Lenape would be known as the Delaware Indians.

It was only a matter of time before whites would arrive. When the tall mast of their ship first appeared to the Lenape in 1638, the last journal entry was made into the Wallam Olum. And what it said was both chilling and prophetic, because it captured the whole of everything in the future of Indian-white contact:

Who are they?[6]

WHAT HAPPENED TO THE LENAPE?

What happened to the Lenni Lenape happened to many tribal nations as they came into contact with the Europeans. They had no resistance to European diseases like measles, chicken pox, and smallpox. Fourteen epidemics struck them after 1633 and reduced their numbers by 90 percent. Alcohol, one of the goods traded by the Europeans for furs, almost destroyed their culture. They were forced to move by the colonists, or the new American government. Many moved back to the Ohio River Valley. Some eventually moved west to Missouri. A small group settled in east Texas. Another small group ended up in Wisconsin, where they joined with a group of Mohican, another Lenape-speaking people, to form the community of Stockbridge-Munsee. Some of them were forced to move and found homes in Kansas and Oklahoma.

The Lenape (Delaware) didn't disappear. They remain with us today, scattered in numbers that exceed thirteen thousand people across the United States. And they remain an important part of the Ojibwe past, for the Lenape are our Grandfathers. We honor the Ancient Ones as we *honor our elders.*

ACTIVITIES

GOOD PATH PROJECTS

- Interview an elder (a grandparent, an uncle or aunt, or an elderly person you know and respect) to learn about his or her life.

- Many tribes relied on the oral tradition (the telling of stories and teachings using spoken stories) rather than written stories. List all the ways that oral stories might be useful in keeping an account of historical events. List the ways that written stories are useful.

- Wampum shells were used as currency (money) by the Lenni Lenape and other tribes. Use books and the computer to learn what objects other people in the world used as money before paper money and coins were used.

- Part of the story told in the Wallam Olum may have occurred during the last Ice Age. Use books and the computer to learn what life was like for people during the last Ice Age.

- The Lenni Lenape migration moved from the west to the east, across the Northwest Coast, Great Plateau, Great Plains, Mississippi Valley, Ohio Valley, and Delaware Valley. Use books and the computer to learn how geography and climate (weather) might have affected the lifestyle, economy, and culture of tribes living in these regions.

- Use books and the computer to learn how tribes related by culture and language to the Ojibwe (such as the Ottawa, Passamaquaddy, and Penobscot) are similar to the Ojibwe. How are they different?

In one dream, my daughter comes to the door. She is young, maybe four or five years old. I need to remind myself that she was just sixteen when she completed the circle of her time on this Earth. "Daddy," she bubbles, "do you want to come out in the pasture and play with us?" I look out the door to see her beautiful dark eyes sparkle, and there behind her in the yard are my two boys. Both are also young, maybe four or five years old, and I know them now to be adults. All of them are wearing bib overalls, the kind I wore when I was young. We run across the yard and I lift the barbed wire of the pasture fence, and they duck under it and run into the open spaces. "Hurry up," they laugh. I duck under the wire and enter the pasture. Then I stand there, looking down at myself. Bib overalls. Small child hands. Little guy. And I am wearing my big shoes with the laces that hook. Off we run.

—Thomas Peacock

HONOR WOMEN

CHAPTER THREE

Grandmother Moon

This is an old story about the first woman. For countless generations, it was told to young people when they sat around the campfires of the ancient villages of the Ojibwe. And in the telling of the story, young people were reminded to *honor women.* Maybe when you are an adult, you will tell it to your children, nieces and nephews, or grandchildren. In that way, the story will go on forever.

FIRST WOMAN

The first of all mothers was a spirit who lived in the sky. She gave birth to two children, twins. One was a spirit and the other was like us in many ways, a physical being. Because they were so different, the twins fought and eventually destroyed each other. For a long time after that, the first woman lived alone. Then the Creator sent her a companion and she conceived (became pregnant) again. Her companion left and she was alone again. Some of the creatures of the Earth noticed her in her loneliness and they asked her to join them on the Earth.

At first her only company were the animal beings. Then the children she had conceived were born. One was a girl and the other was a boy. They were different from her last children. Both were made of physical substances (water and earth), yet each had a soul-spirit (a soul). Their soul-spirits had the ability to dream and to have visions. These new people were called *Anishinaabeg,* meaning "spontaneous beings." They were the Earth's first humans.

For many years, the first of all mothers lived on the Earth with her children and the animals. When she was satisfied they could survive on their own, she told them

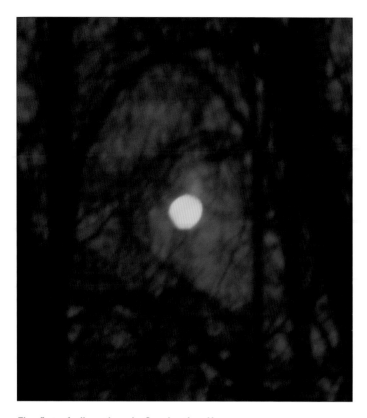

The first of all mothers is Grandmother Moon.

first of Mothers, Nokomis (Grandmother), whenever the moon gave light. At the same time, they remembered the primacy of women, who bore the unique gift of life, for it was through woman that the cycle—creation, destruction, recreation—was completed.[7]

So the first of all mothers is Grandmother Moon. At night she shines down on the Ojibwe, offering her love and comfort to the people. Her light helps guide humans on their journeys through life.

MOTHER EARTH

she would return to the sky, the land of peace. She told them that when their time on Earth was complete, their soul-spirits would join her there. That is why we Ojibwe believe that all of us go to the land of peace when we pass on to the spirit world:

Then the Spirit woman ascended into the sky to return to her home. Thereafter, the Anishinabeg remembered the

In the order of things, the Ojibwe saw the sun as the father. To pay respect to the father, all the lodges in the ancient villages were built facing the east, to the rising sun. Tobacco *(asema)* was offered in prayer to the rising and setting sun. In rising, the sun gave life through its warmth and energy; in setting, the sun gave plants and animals time to sleep. Sunlight was needed to sustain life, working in conjunction with the Earth.

Earth is the mother to all of the creatures, including humankind. All of us are made of earth. All the flowers in their beauty are born and spring from the earth. All the grasses and trees do the same. All creatures gain nourishment from the earth. And as they age and wither and die, all living things return to the earth, their mother. Like all children, all living things are born from and seek the comfort of their mother. And, like all children, all living things love the Earth. The Earth lives on forever.

Earth is the mother of all of the creatures, including humankind. All of us are made of earth.

THE SEASONAL CYCLE OF WOMEN

Life in traditional Ojibwe villages had women's work, men's work, and work they shared. In those times, all work was of equal value. No job was unimportant. Each had unique purposes and reasons for being.

Village life followed the seasons. In the spring, the people went to the sugar bush to harvest maple syrup. Birch-bark baskets were taken out of storage and used to collect the maple sap. The women and girls tapped the trees while the men and boys gathered firewood and ice-fished. Women and girls would clean the fish

An Ojibwe girl becomes a woman.

and hang them on a twig frame over a fire to dry. The women would open storage pits where the previous fall they had put food: bags of wild rice, potatoes, and dried apples and blueberries, pin cherries, chokecherries, gooseberries, and cranberries. The berries would be mixed and eaten with the new maple syrup. Everyone worked to boil the sap into maple sugar, taffy, and sugar cakes. During this time, the women also gathered the inside bark of cedar for making mats and bags. Later in the spring, the Ojibwe would move to their summer camp and care for their gardens. Men would break the ground with wooden and bone hoes made from the shoulder blades of large deer or moose. Women planted pumpkins, squash, corn, and beans. Women and young girls would gather wild potatoes and, later on, all of the summer berries (strawberries, blueberries, Juneberries, and gooseberries). They made cedar-bark mats and cedar bags to store things in. Birch bark and basswood bark were gathered for making containers and covering lodges, and the birch bark was also used in canoe-building. Later in the summer, the women and girls also gathered reeds for making mats. The older women gathered the herbs used as medicines, bringing the younger children along as they collected their precious harvest.

In the fall, the people would move to wild-rice camps. Women would tie the rice in bunches as it stood in the lakes so it would be easier to harvest. The ties for each family were different so they could identify the area of the lake they would make (gather) wild rice. Men and women harvested and made rice together. Then they would return to their summer camps to harvest their gardens

In earlier times, all work was of equal value. There was no job that was unimportant.

Women and girls gathered reeds for making mats.

and to store things for the upcoming winter. Also in the fall, men would go trapping and hunting to make sure there was plenty of meat for the winter season. Women would do the fall fishing and dry the fish for storage.

Then they would move to winter camp, which was always close to the hunting areas. The men would hunt and trap for the larger animals, and the women would clean and dry the meat over the fires. Women and girls snared rabbits and partridge. They also cleaned and tanned animal hides, and they made and repaired moccasins, mittens, and fishing nets.

And in the spring, the circle of the seasons would begin all over again.

THE ROLE OF WOMEN AS LEADERS, TEACHERS, AND HEALERS

Women and men were members of the council of leaders, generally elders, in Ojibwe villages. This council chose one member to be the overall leader. Few decisions could be made without the leader gaining the approval of the council. The council decided on the movement

Ojibwe women made birch-bark baskets for storage and to hold maple sap.

the girls would go with the older women to be taught the ways of women, and the boys would go with men to be taught men's ways. The skills of living were taught (gardening, fishing, building lodges, making clothing), and the teachers also talked to the young about looking into their hearts to discover their inner being. So education consisted of two phases: One was to teach young people the skills of living, and the other was to instruct them on the path to wisdom. "The true wisdom you seek lies deep in your heart," the teachers would say.

A woman parches wild rice.

to the different seasonal camps and the distribution of the hunting and fishing areas inside and outside the community. The council also settled individual and family disputes and made the important decisions of war and peace.

Grandmothers, aunties, and older sisters cared for the very young while the women and men worked. Later,

And, in saying that, they meant that wisdom came from living out the values of the Good Path.

Women and men were healers, or medicine people. Young children who showed promise as healers were trained in the vocation by medicine women and men. From them, children learned of the healing plants. They would go deep into the forests with the medicine people to learn to find and gather the plants. They also learned the songs that would be sung and the prayers that would be said in the healing ceremonies.

Women served as teachers, medicine people, and members on the council of leaders.

THE ROLE OF OJIBWE WOMEN AFTER THE COMING OF EUROPEAN SETTLERS

One of the greatest debts Ojibwe people owe women came during the difficult time that followed the coming of European settlers. This was a time when the people

Ojibwe women held families together during the difficult period following the coming of European settlers.

became lost physically, emotionally, and spiritually. All the confusion following the coming of the white people threatened to break families and communities apart, and it was women who held the families together. When men lost their roles as family provider, women stepped into that role. They cultivated large gardens and worked in town jobs for the white settlers so there was food to put on the table. They kept the home together when men had to leave to work in lumber camps and on farms. They kept families together when some men turned to alcohol. They raised children when some men abandoned their families. They continued to teach the old ways when some men were no longer there to teach. And they kept alive the old stories as reminders of who we are as Ojibwe people. Here, a grandmother teaches an important lesson to her granddaughter:

When the forest weeps, the Anishinabe who listen will look back over the years. In each generation of Ojibway, there will be a person who will hear the si-si-gwa-d [the murmuring of the trees when the branches rub against each other], who will listen and remember and pass it on to their children. Remembering our past and acting accordingly will ensure that we, the Ojibway, will always people the earth.[8]

Winona LaDuke is a White Earth Ojibwe, author, and activist.

OJIBWE WOMEN OF TODAY

Today's Ojibwe women are leaders in tribal governments, doctors, teachers, attorneys, and businesspeople. They are modern warriors who help make certain that the Ojibwe people have a voice in this country. Most are mothers as well.

While many outstanding women live in Ojibwe country, two deserve special mention. Winona LaDuke, a White Earth Ojibwe, ran for vice president of the United States in 2000. Louise Erdrich, a Turtle Mountain Ojibwe, is one of America's foremost writers.

But Ojibwe women at all levels are doing important work in their communities. They work at our powwows, visit the ill and elderly, and organize events to serve those in need. They are our mothers, grandmothers, aunties, sisters, wives, and daughters. We *honor* them.

We honor women.

ACTIVITIES

GOOD PATH PROJECTS

♦ Identify a girl or woman you hold in great respect. Interview that person and write a story about her.

♦ Use books and the computer to learn how some cultures treat women and men differently.
Are there cultures where the roles are considered unequal?
Are there cultures where women hold the dominant roles?
Are women and men treated equally in modern America?

♦ Use books and the computer to learn about contemporary Ojibwe women, including activist Winona LaDuke and author Louise Erdrich.

For most of my life, I lived in Fond du Lac on the land of my ancestors—
my grandparents, mother, aunts, and uncles. I am so much a part
of the circle of that place. When I walk that land—the hills and fields
that overlook the river that flows through Nahgachiwanong (place where
the water stops)—I walk the same paths as they did. And the very earth
that greets me with all its simple beauty is the same earth that provided
for them. The grandparents of the bears I have seen presented
themselves to my grandparents. The ancestors of the fish I have caught
from the river presented themselves when my ancestors fished the river.
This is such a sacred journey I am a part of; it goes on forever.

—Thomas Peacock

CHAPTER FOUR

The Prophecies

Many cultures have prophecies (predictions about the future). The Hopi tribe, for example, had prophecies predicting missions to outer space and space stations. Bible prophecies predicted a new nation of Israel, which became a reality in 1948. The Ojibwe also have prophecies about the future. One is the Seven Fires prophecies, a series of ancient predictions about our people that have come true. There are many teachings in the Seven Fires prophecies, and one important one is to *honor our elder brothers, the plant and animal beings.*

Sometimes predictions about the future can become self-fulfilling prophecies. In other words, because we know the prediction, we may work to make it come true. For example, people might say bad things about a young person, such as, "That kid is such a troublemaker." And the young person who hears he is a troublemaker might just make some trouble. This is especially true if he hears it often enough and from enough people. Eventually he might believe it. And he could grow up to be a troublemaker because that is what people expect of him and what he expects of himself. Likewise, the opposite could happen. If young people hear a lot of good things said about them, they often become adults who live in a good way.

No one knows to what degree the Seven Fires prophecies are self-fulfilling, but the predictions made by the Ojibwe prophets go a long way toward explaining what has happened to our people through the ages.

THE OJIBWE VIEW OF THE NATURAL WORLD

To understand the meaning of the Seven Fires prophecies, humankind must understand how the Ojibwe see nature, especially our beliefs about plants and animals. Knowing how we view plants and animals will help humans better understand the last two prophecies.

THE PLANT BEINGS

The Creator made the Earth first, followed by the plants. Plants can live without animals or people. They depend only on the physical properties of the earth and sky (water, earth, sunlight, and heat) to exist. Through the remarkable process of photosynthesis, plants can convert light from our sun into energy. Plants also draw minerals directly from the earth and from water. And plants come in all shapes, sizes, colors, and textures imaginable, from giant redwoods to tiny wildflowers. The Ojibwe believe that each plant has its own soul. Even more remarkable, each plant soul can join with other plants to create a collective soul:

Each valley or any other earth form—a meadow, a bay, a hill—possesses a mood which reflects the state of being of that place. Whatever the mood, happy, peaceful, turbulent, or melancholy, it is the tone of that soul-

spirit. As proof, destroy or alter or remove a portion of the plant beings, and the mood and tone of that valley will not be what it was before.[9]

Tobacco *(asema)* is used as a ceremonial substance to help communicate with the Creator.

A culture that believes plants have souls would not purposely destroy them. Plants, like all life forms, are sacred beings. Each has an important purpose as a part of creation. Plants serve as food for animals and humans, as medicine, and as ceremonial substances to help communicate with the Creator. Tobacco *(asema)*, cedar, and sweetgrass are examples of ceremonial substances. The smoke of tobacco is used to transport humankind's thoughts to the Creator. Cedar is used in Ojibwe ceremonial lodges. It is burned, along with sweetgrass, to purify.

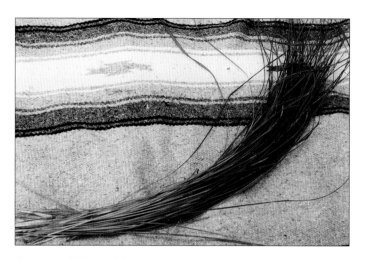

Sweetgrass *(wiingashk)* is used for purification.

THE ANIMAL BEINGS

After the Creator made the plant beings, the animal beings were created. Animals depend on plants and the physical earth and sky (earth, water, wind, sunlight, and heat) for their existence. Because they were created before humankind, animal and plant beings are referred to as our elder brothers. Animals were given unique powers. One of their powers is precognition (sometimes called the sixth sense), which is the ability to sense things before they happen. For example, some animals can sense storms before they happen. Each animal was created for a special purpose, and each has some of the Creator's nature (the Creator's ways). Dogs love unconditionally without expecting to be loved in return. Snakes keep the fields and meadows clean. Bears represent strength. It was the animals that saved the world after the flood. It was the muskrat that sacrificed itself to get a piece of the old Earth upon which the new Earth was created.

Humankind depends on animals for food and clothing, and also for their unique knowledge of the world. When our Ojibwe ancestors wanted to know when the seasons were about to change, for example, they would watch the animals. They knew that summer was changing to fall when birds began gathering in large groups and started their migration. Squirrels would begin storing food. Bears would fatten up for their hibernation. And because animals were given some of the Creator's character, we can learn much by watching how they live their lives. Gulls represent peace and grace. Cranes represent eloquence and leadership. Wolves represent perseverance (the ability to stick to something and not quit) and guardianship.

Animals had enormous importance in traditional Ojibwe society. Families and villages were organized by *dodaim,* sometimes called *totem,* or clans, represented by an animal. These clans had special functions. There were originally seven dodaim in Ojibwe society. Marriage within clans was not allowed. Clan membership was determined along the father's line (the father's clan determined the children's clan). These are the seven original clans of the Ojibwe and what they represent:

CLAN	FUNCTION
Crane *(Ah-ji-jawk')*	leadership
Bear *(Mu-kwa)*	police and herbal-medicine people
Marten *(Wa-bi-zha-shi)*	sustenance (survival)
Fish *(Gi-goon)*	learning
Loon *(Mahng)*	leadership
Deer *(Wa-wa-shesh'-she)*	gentle people
Bird *(Be-nays')*	spiritual leaders[10]

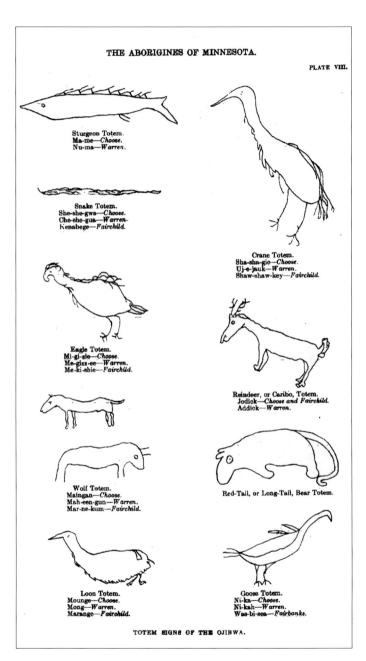

Animals represented ***dodaim,*** or clans, of the Ojibwe.

The crane represented leadership and eloquence.

THE SEVEN FIRES PROPHECIES

Many centuries ago, when the Ojibwe lived on the Atlantic Ocean, seven spirits came among the people and foretold the future of the tribe. These prophecies are called the Seven Fires.

The first prophet told the people they would eventually move to the west, following the sacred *Megis* shell (a small seashell). After the Lenni Lenape, the Ojibwe people's ancient ancestors, had made a great eastward migration generations before, why would they now begin a westward journey? They did so because

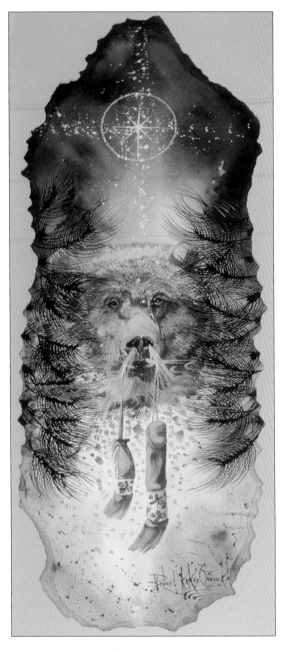

Bears represent strength.

they were told if they didn't migrate, they would be destroyed.

On their journey the Ojibwe would make seven stops. Their first and final stops would be at turtle-shaped islands. When the Ojibwe did make their westward migration, the first stop may have been one of two islands along the St. Lawrence River, near present-day Montreal, Canada. The final stop was Madeline Island, just offshore the present-day northern-Wisconsin Ojibwe community of Red Cliff. The first prophet also said:

You will know that the chosen ground has been reached when you come to a land where food grows on water. If you do not move, you will be destroyed.[11]

The food that grows on water is wild rice, an edible grass that grows naturally in parts of Minnesota, Wisconsin, and southern Canada. And some of the people did stay rather than take part in the westward migration. These people were almost destroyed by war and the diseases brought to the continent by the Europeans. Wayne Newell is a Passamaquaddy elder from Maine whose tribe had nearly been destroyed by early contact with whites. When asked if his tribe had stories

"You will know that the chosen ground has been reached when you come to a land where food [wild rice] grows on water." (**Eddie Benton-Banai,** *The Mishomis Book*)

about when the Ojibwe lived among them on the Atlantic Coast, he said: "We stayed. We sent you west. We felt that the only way to save our culture was to send some people west."

The second prophet told the people that during the Second Fire, the people would be living near a large body of water. The spiritual beliefs of the Ojibwe would not be practiced in a way that would satisfy the Creator, but a young boy would be born who would lead the people back to living the Good Path. The second stopping-place was near present-day Niagara Falls.

The third prophet told the people they would find the path to their new homelands in the west, in the place where food grew on water. The Ojibwe migration followed the great water highway along the Great Lakes, which today is a major shipping route for raw materials from the Midwest. Iron, wheat, corn, and other goods produced in the Midwest travel in large ships to cities along the East Coast and all over the world. The third stopping-place was probably near the Detroit River, near the junction of Lake Erie and Lake Huron.

The fourth prophet appeared as two spirits and predicted the coming of Europeans to the Americas. The spirits gave a warning, which in time was to come true. The first spirit said:

You will know the future of our people by the face the Light-skinned race wears. If they come wearing the face of brotherhood, then there will come a time of wonderful change for generations to come . . .

The other spirit continued:

Beware if the Light-skinned race comes wearing the face of death. You must be careful because the face of broth-

The Ojibwe followed the sacred Megis shell on their westward journey.

erhood and the face of death look very much alike. If they come carrying a weapon . . . beware. If they come in suffering . . . they could fool you. Their hearts may be filled with greed for the riches of this land.[12]

Because our ancestors mistook the face of death for the face of brotherhood, the Ojibwe people (and most tribal people of the Americas) have suffered for many generations. Whole tribes died out from warfare and disease. Whole nations were wiped off the face of the Earth.

The fifth prophet said the people would move away from their ancient spiritual ways, which came true as many Ojibwe became Christianized.

Ojibwe people honor plants in this beaded apron.

The sixth prophet told of a time of great suffering for Ojibwe people, when many would lose their way emotionally, physically, spiritually, and psychologically. We know that a period of great difficulty came upon our great-grandparents, grandparents, parents, and some of our current generation. Our language was nearly taken from us in boarding schools. Alcoholism and drug use became huge problems in many of our communities. So did physical and sexual abuse. Families have been broken. Individuals' spirits have been stripped of their pride because of poverty and all the ills that come with being

poor. All of this has gone on for generations. And the Ojibwe are just now beginning to recover from the time of the Sixth Fire.

Then the seventh prophet came among the people. He was young and had a "strange light in his eyes."[13] He predicted that in the time of the Seventh Fire, young people (called the new people) would try to regain what they had lost. They would try to return to living the culture and following the Good Path. But it would

The animal beings are honored in this quill-and-sweetgrass box.

be a difficult road because many elders would also be lost or afraid to give the new people direction. These people, *Osh-ki-bi-ma-di-zeeg*, would have the potential to lead the Ojibwe back to being a great and powerful people and to a wondrous time for the people of the Earth. But it will eventually be the white race that will be given a choice to make, and their decision will ultimately decide the fate of humankind on Earth:

It is at this time that the Light-skinned Race will be given a choice between two roads. If they choose the right road, then the Seventh Fire will light the Eighth and Final Fire— an eternal Fire of peace, love, brotherhood, and sisterhood. If the Light-skinned race makes the wrong choice of roads, then the destruction which they brought with them in coming to this country will come back to them and cause much suffering and death to all the Earth's people.[14]

To many traditional Ojibwe people, the meaning of the final prophecy is clear. If humans *honor our elder brothers* (the plant and animal beings) and all the things of this Earth, we will be rewarded with an eternally wondrous time. But if we continue to pollute the Earth and deplete it of its precious resources without giving back, then all of humankind will suffer. If we believe that plants

The Earth itself is a sacred place, a place to be forever treasured.

and animals are sacred beings that were given some of Creator's power and nature, then we are obligated to protect them. The Earth is a sacred place, a place to be forever treasured.

ACTIVITIES

TEST YOUR MEMORY

- What are the seven original Ojibwe clans?
  What do they represent?

- Plants and animals were considered elder brothers in traditional Ojibwe society because they were created before humankind. List the physical characteristics we share with animals.
  What kinds of emotions do we share with animals?
  What kinds of languages do they speak, and how might we understand what the different sounds they make mean?
  List the physical characteristics we share with plants. How do we rely on plants for food, shelter, medicine, and beauty?

- Many cultures had prophets and prophecies. Use books and the computer to find examples of each.
  How are the prophecies similar?
  How are they different?

- What are your favorite plant and favorite animal?
  What is it about each that makes it your favorite?
  What are the characteristics of the animal that you admire?
  Make a drawing or painting of your animal or write a poem or story about it.

- Use books and the computer to learn about animals like pigs, dogs, the higher primates (chimpanzees, orangutans, gorillas), whales, dolphins and porpoises, crows, and parrots.
  What do scientists know about the intelligence of these creatures?
  What do we know about the ways they think and what they understand?

Some years ago, I drove back from the East Coast with my younger brother. I had lived away from my home community of Fond du Lac for nearly two decades. As we neared the reservation, I became apprehensive. I wondered what it would be like to again live in the land of my ancestors, remembered only through my childhood eyes. Just as I wondered these things, there, spread out before me, was the blue expanse of Lake Superior. It embraced me like an Ojibwe grandmother, holding me and comforting my soul. And I said in barely a whisper, yet in a voice that resounded over the earth and sky of my childhood, "I am home. I am home."

—Thomas Peacock

CHAPTER FIVE

The Westward Migration

This is the story of the Ojibwe's westward migration from Canada and the area of Newfoundland and New Brunswick where the St. Lawrence River enters the Atlantic Ocean. The journey may have begun nearly eleven hundred years ago and taken nearly five hundred years to complete. Our ancestors finally settled on what is known today as Madeline Island in Lake Superior, just offshore of Red Cliff, Wisconsin. The westward migration took them into the lands of other tribes, and, although wars resulted from entering those lands, for the most part the Ojibwe learned to *be peaceful* with them.

BEGINNING THE JOURNEY

You will remember it was the prophet of the First Fire who told the Ojibwe they would move west. Following the appearance of the prophets of the Seven Fires, there was much debate among the people. At the time, the Ojibwe and their Lenape relatives lived in great communities up and down the East Coast, from southern Canada into New England and down into Virginia. Life was good. They raised crops of corn, squash, and beans. They fished the nearby ocean, lakes, and streams. The great forests of the eastern woodlands were teeming with animals, which offered themselves to the people as food. The Ojibwe lived in harmony with their Lenape neighbors and had a flourishing trade with the Lenape and other tribes.

For the most part, they lived in peace. War between the Ojibwe and other tribes was infrequent. The fights of the young warriors were usually not intended to end with killing someone. Fighting was more a test of skill and strength, and to put one's self in danger was a great test of courage. To be sure, warriors were injured and some were killed. When that happened, the warriors wanted to seek vengeance. Elders would always try, sometimes in vain, to convince warriors of the folly of war and of the need to *be peaceful.*

Although they were a large and powerful nation, the Ojibwe were uneasy at the thought of moving to a strange new land. What would their new home be like? Would the new home provide for them as well as the place in which they lived? When they encountered

new people, would these people be friendly to them? The Ojibwe knew it would be a long journey that would last many generations. And they knew that the people might never find the new homeland spoken of by the prophets.

"Why should we move from this place? We live a good life here," many said.

"But we need to listen to the prophets," said others. They remembered what the prophet of the First Fire

The Ojibwe ended their westward migration on the shores surrounding the blue expanse of Lake Superior.

had told them: if they didn't migrate, they would be destroyed. The wise ones also knew that, long ago, their Lenape ancestors had lived in the west and that the migration would take them back to their old homelands.

So the debate went on until it was finally decided that some would stay, and the great body of people would move. Plans were made. Preparations began. Dried berries, vegetables, pemmican (dried and seasoned meat), smoked fish, and nuts, all of which had been stored, were packed for traveling. Birch-bark canoes were repaired and new ones made. Wigwams were taken down, and the hides and bark that covered them were carefully wrapped and put on travois (sleds made with two poles and pulled by dogs) for moving. The most difficult thing to do was to say good-bye to neighbors, friends, and their Lenape relatives, whom they would never see again.

The people kept an eternal fire, the Sacred Fire. It was a symbol of the strength of their spiritual beliefs and a reminder of their identity as tribal people. It was kept burning during the five hundred years of their journey. Embers of the fire were carefully wrapped within thick leather and kept by the fire keepers.

When the journey began, there was an uneasy sense among the people leaving. They felt that those who stayed would have great difficulties in the future, and that was to come true. The Wampanoag, our Lenape relatives who met the Pilgrims when they landed at Plymouth Rock, died by the thousands from the introduction of European diseases. They would try to defend their homelands from settlers moving onto their land, and a great war would be fought. Being no match for the Pilgrims' muskets and cannons, the Wampanoag

The debate went on until it was finally decided that some would stay and the great body of people would move.

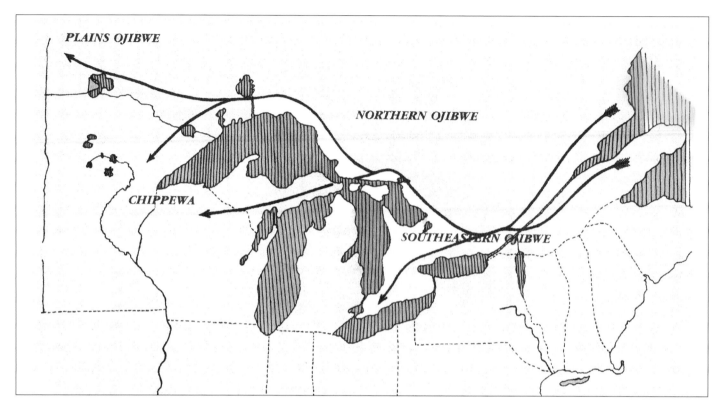

The migration route of the Ojibwe led them through and around the Great Lakes region.

were slaughtered. Some were sold into slavery and shipped to the islands of the Caribbean, never returning to their homelands. The Grandfathers, the Delaware, would suffer greatly from their contact with the Europeans. The Nantascot, a Lenape tribe that lived in what is known today as Boston Harbor, would vanish forever from the face of the earth. Other tribes would also vanish.

The first prophet had told the Ojibwe that they would make seven stops, and that the first and last stops would be at turtle-shaped islands. The prophet also said they would be led on their journey by a sacred Megis shell (the cowrie, a small seashell). At each stop, it would rise. And it would set when the time came for the people to continue their journey. The Megis shell is still used in the spiritual practices of traditional Ojibwe people.

The journey began with the Ojibwe, Ottawa, and Po-towatomi people, then one nation of Anishinaabeg. Later along the journey, they would separate and become their own tribal nations.

THE TURTLE-SHAPED ISLAND

The tribal people traveled by canoe and foot westward along the St. Lawrence River, living out the prophecy of

The first stop was a turtle-shaped island near present-day Montreal, Canada.

the Seven Fires. Their first stop was a turtle-shaped island near present-day Montreal, Canada, called *Mo-ne-aung* in the Ojibwe language. To this day, the Ojibwe disagree about which island the people settled. Some Ojibwe say it was an island just to the east of present-day Montreal, where the St. Frances River flows into the St. Lawrence River. Others say it was an island at the junction of the Ottawa and St. Lawrence Rivers. It may never be known.

What is known is that the islands near Montreal were often visited by many tribal nations. Here the people stayed in a great village for many years. But eventually many of them remembered it was their destiny (life mission) to continue their westward journey, so they moved on. At each stop in the journey, some stayed behind. To this day, there are tribal people living all along the St. Lawrence River and throughout the Great Lakes region whose ancestors were part of the great migration.

THE GREAT FALLS

The second stop was at Niagara Falls, located on the Niagara River that connects the St. Lawrence River with the first of the Great Lakes, Lake Erie. Niagara Falls, called *Kichi-ka-be-kong* (Great Falls), must have been a place of great awe and wonder for the travelers. The mist of Niagara Falls always shows a rainbow on sunny days. And the thundering roar of the water as it crashes onto the rocks below must have reminded the people of the water's great power. And again, just as it did at the first stop, the Megis shell was said to have risen from the horizon.

Eventually, the Megis shell set and did not rise again until the people reached the Detroit River, which connects Lake Erie and Lake Huron. Crossing the river was difficult because of the swift current and rapids. During this time, the tribes began to divide into groups to form the Three Fires Confederacy. One group would become known as the Potowatomi, the keepers of the Sacred Fire. It was their responsibility to ensure that the coals of the nation's sacred fire would never die. The second group became known as the Ottawa, or traders. Their responsibility was to lead trading efforts and hunting expeditions. The third group, the keepers of the spiritual beliefs, kept the name Ojibwe. Brotherhood and sisterhood are still strong today among the people of the Three Fires.

All along the way the travelers encountered tribal nations, including the Fox, Sauk, Dakota, Iroquois, and Menominee. The Ojibwe tried to live in peace with all of these nations. Conflict was inevitable, though, because the Ojibwe were treading on others' gathering (agricultural and hunting) lands. Battles were fought, and the Ojibwe would eventually win those wars.

Peace would finally come, one by one, with all of these tribes. Each of these nations would eventually become

The second stop was at Niagara Falls.

Mackinac Island, near the fourth stop of the migration, overlooks Lake Michigan.

our friend, and trading and commerce would flow freely among the tribal nations.

MANITOULIN ISLAND

The prophet of the Second Fire had predicted that many Ojibwe would move away from their spiritual practices for a period, but that a young boy would lead them back onto the Good Path. The Ojibwe had traveled along the north end of Lake Huron until they came to Georgian Bay. They didn't know how to get across such a large body of water. A young boy had a dream of stepping-stones (islands) that would lead them across the water and on to the west. The people followed the dream of the boy. The largest of these islands was Manitoulin, and it became the fourth stop on the journey. Today, bands of Ojibwe, Potowatomi, and Ottawa people still live on the island.

THE OJIBWE SEPARATE AT SAULT SAINTE MARIE

The westward journey continued, leading the tribal people to *Ba-wa-ting* (rapids in a river), now known as Sault Sainte Marie. While here at the fifth stop, the Ojibwe would eventually split into two groups. One group went west along the south shore of Lake Superior. The other went north around the big lake until they reached Spirit Island, located in St. Louis River Bay at Duluth, Minnesota. For the Ojibwe, Spirit Island would be the sixth stop along their journey. Here they found wild rice, the food that grows on water, and the prophecy of the First Fire was fulfilled. It was at Spirit Island that the northern travelers and the southern group joined up again:

The Northern division formed the least numerous body and consisted chiefly of the families claiming as Totems the rein-

Here at *Ba-wa-ting* (rapids in the river) the Ojibwe would eventually split into two groups. One group went west along the south shore of Lake Superior, while the other went north around the lake.

deer, lynx, and pike. They proceeded gradually to occupy the north coast of Lake Superior, till they arrived at the mouth of Pigeon River. . . . From this point, they have spread over the country they occupy at the present day. . . .

The main body pressed their way gradually along the southern shores of Lake Superior. They made a temporary stand at Grand Island, near the Pictured Rocks, again at L'Anse Bay. . . . This grand division consisted principally of the Crane Totem family, the Bear, the Catfish, the Loon, and the allied Marten and Moose clans. These large families with their several branches form at least eight-tenths of the whole Ojibway tribe.[15]

The Ottawa and Potowatomi would also settle into their own communities at this time. The Ottawa would remain near Sault Sainte Marie, and the Potowatomi would settle in what is today northern Michigan and parts of Wisconsin.

Some Ojibwe must have felt their arrival at Spirit Island meant they had reached their final destination. Others wondered and asked aloud, "Where is the turtle-shaped island we were to find for our final destination?" The people of the southern group remembered an island just to the east, and the main body of Ojibwe continued their great migration. They found and settled on *Moningwanakining,* the place of the yellow-breasted woodpecker, now known as Wisconsin's Madeline Island. The great Ojibwe nation made its home on Madeline Island for many years to come.

Surrounded by the deep blue of Lake Superior, they felt protected from the nearby Fox and Dakota tribes. The great westward migration of the Ojibwe was complete. And there they found peace and lived out the value of *being peaceful.*

Spirit Island on the St. Louis River was the sixth stop of the migration.

ACTIVITIES

- Why did the Ojibwe migrate from the Atlantic Ocean?
  What were their reasons for staying or leaving?
  What kinds of difficulties do you think the Ojibwe encountered along the migration?
  How do you think they overcame them?
  What do you think happened to the people who stayed behind instead of migrating?

- Why was peace sometimes interrupted during the westward migration of the Ojibwe?
  What kinds of things lead to conflict among people and nations?
  What kinds of things lead to peace?
  Why is peace so difficult to maintain?

GOOD PATH PROJECTS

- The Great Lakes are important to the United States and Canada for shipping, tourism, and recreation. Use books and the computer to learn about one of the lakes and how it influences the people and communities that live along its shores. Create a map of the lake.

- There have been other important migrations of people during the history of humankind (the migration of humans out of Africa throughout the rest of the world, the migration of Europeans to the Americas, the settlement of the American West). Use books and the computer to learn why people move to different places.

- Use books and the computer to learn about one of the seven stopping places along the Ojibwe migration (Montreal, Niagara Falls, Detroit, Manitoulin Island, Sault Sainte Marie, Duluth, and Madeline Island) and how the people live there today.

Now in the third hill of my life, I find myself drawn back to those sacred islands, the Apostle Islands. In the dark quiet of the forests, I have heard the si-si-gwad (the murmuring of the trees when their branches touch each other). The whole story of our people is contained in that sound.

—Thomas Peacock

CHAPTER SIX

The Place of the Yellow-Breasted Woodpecker

Imagine our Ojibwe ancestors when *Moningwanakining* (Madeline Island, the place of the yellow-breasted woodpecker) came into view for the first time, and they saw the homeland described so many generations ago by the prophets of the Seventh Fire. Imagine our great nation paddling to the island in their birch-bark canoes. They were a nation just like we Ojibwe are today—with elders, fathers and mothers, aunties and uncles, cousins, warriors, medicine people and spiritual leaders, teens, children, and babies. Our ancestors carried with them all of their possessions. And they made that long and dangerous journey that spanned many generations only because they cooperated with each other as a group and lived out the value of *being kind to everyone.*

It was said that the sacred Megis shell, which had led them all the way from their eastern homeland, rose for the final time over Madeline Island. Imagine yourself fi-nally arriving home after a journey that took centuries. If you can, then you know the joy that our Ojibwe ancestors felt. Madeline Island is the Ojibwe people's sacred homeland, the place of our creation, our Turtle Island:

Madeline Island is our tribal home, the place where the earth began, the place that first came back from the flood. Naanabozho [Waynabozho], the trickster, was born here, on this island. . . . This is our place on the earth, this place is in our bodies, in our words, and in our dreams.[16]

THE APOSTLE ISLANDS

On northern Wisconsin's northernmost point lies an archipelago (a grouping) of twenty-one islands in the deep blue of Lake Superior. Named the Apostle Islands by the first French explorers (because they thought there were only twelve islands), it remains a remote, lightly settled, and hauntingly beautiful place.

The Apostle Islands were created some twelve thousand years ago, when ice moved over much of glacial Lake Superior. When the glacier receded, the islands remained. Each is unique. Eagle Island, for instance, is the home of nesting bald eagles. Sand Island has sea caves carved by wave action into its brownstone shoreline. Sand, Raspberry, Michigan, and Devil's Islands have lighthouses. Oak Island has high hills from which you can view the other islands. Basswood and Hermit

The Ojibwe settled the village of LaPointe on Madeline Island.

Islands have abandoned quarries that once provided the brownstone used for buildings in Duluth, Chicago, Milwaukee, and other midwestern cities. Stockton Island has one of the largest concentrations of black bears in the country. Madeline is the largest of the islands. Fourteen miles long and three miles wide, it has a year-round population of only 180 people. That population grows to nearly twenty-five hundred in the summer tourist season.

Sunrise breaks over Madeline Island.

THE OJIBWE SETTLE ON MADELINE ISLAND

When the Ojibwe arrived at the Apostle Islands, they temporarily settled on Long Island, a short distance from Madeline. It was not a safe place for permanent settlement. They were attacked by the Dakota and Fox, who lived in the area, so they moved to the larger island of Madeline. At that time, Madeline was covered with a virgin forest of hemlock, white pine, and large stands of oak, maple, and basswood. They settled on its westward shore in a place known later as LaPointe and built a large village, covering two miles by three miles. And they kept the Sacred Fire of the people burning:

During this era of their history, some of their old men affirm that there was maintained in their central town, on the Island of LaPointe, a continual fire as a symbol of their nationality.[17]

LIFE ON MADELINE ISLAND

What was daily life like for the Ojibwe of Madeline Island? How did they live? What did their village look like? What foods did they eat? What were the lives of young people like? And what was it like before and just after the arrival of the first white people among our ancestors? Here is some of what we know.

75

A boy helps prepare wild rice (Mahnomen) for winter storage.

syrup, the maple cakes, and the maple sugar. In the warmth of the late spring, we plant the seed of corn, squash, pumpkin, and beans. In the hotness of the summer, we pick the berries, starting with strawberries, then pin cherries, chokecherries, precious blueberries, and gooseberries. After the blueberry gathering, the harvest begins. The ma-no-min [wild rice] is taken from the lakes, threshed, and stored along with the corn, squash, pumpkin, and beans. Throughout the summer the meat is dried and stored and the herbs and medicine is secured. The fish is dried and the acorns hung. The kin-nik-a-nik [tobacco] is scraped and prepared for daily use.[18]

THE SEASONAL CYCLE

Our ancestors lived according to the cycle of seasons, sunrise to sunrise, full moon to full moon, spring to spring, year to year, birth to death to life again. It is a circle of life that has gone on since the time of creation:

Our life cycle follows the circle designed by Grandmother Earth. In the early spring at the time when the snow turns to water, we go to the sugar bush and make the maple

PLANT HARVESTS

The Ojibwe living on Madeline Island grew several kinds of vegetables. Corn *(mundamin)*, squash, pumpkins, and beans were cultivated in large gardens. Corn was prepared much the way Ojibwe cook it today. It was roasted in its husks over hot coals, parched (roasted) in bark containers, boiled, or dried and saved for later use. Popped corn (popcorn) was a special treat then just as it is now. Pumpkin, squash, and beans were baked or boiled, or dried for later use.

Foods that grew naturally were also harvested and eaten. Wild rice was harvested from nearby lakes and then parched, boiled, or dried. It would become the staple (main) food of the Ojibwe. Maple syrup, taffy, and maple-sugar cakes were made from sugar-maple trees. Teas were made from the leaves and twigs of wintergreen, wild cherry, raspberry, spruce, and snowberry. Pumpkin flowers and corn silk were used to thicken the broth of soups and stews. Bearberry, wild ginger, and mountain mint were used as seasonings. Wild potatoes were eaten, as were the roots of cattails. Acorns were eaten and also made into flour. Berries of all sorts were eaten alone, sometimes sweetened with maple sugar or mixed with the tallow (fat) of deer or moose and used as seasoning. Flowers of various sorts, like the milkweed, were eaten as well.

Many foods were prepared in birch-bark containers. When liquid fills the inside of these leak-proof containers and they are put over a fire, the containers do not burn. The Ojibwe on Madeline Island stored their food in pits dug about six feet deep and lined with birch bark. The tops of the pits were covered with bark or grass, logs, and a mound of dirt.

ANIMAL HARVESTS

Fish of all sorts were harvested by the Ojibwe, who used nets made from nettle twine and who speared and caught fish on bone hooks. The fish were eaten fresh or dried and smoked for later use. Dried fish was prepared by hanging the cleaned fish over a slow-cooking fire or out in the sun. Fish was boiled when it was eaten fresh.

"In the hotness of the summer, we pick the berries, starting with strawberries, then pin cherries, chokecherries, precious blueberries, and gooseberries." (Ignatia Broker, *Night Flying Woman*)

Whitefish, walleye, perch, suckers, northern pike, lake trout, sunfish, and crappies were favorites. Fish eggs were eaten as well, and the heads of some fish, especially suckers, were considered a delicacy (a favorite).

Meat from deer, bear, moose, buffalo, rabbit, and trapped animals of all sorts were harvested and eaten. Beaver tails were a favorite. Meat was eaten fresh or it was dried by first being cut into thin strips and then hung over a low

Fish of all sorts were harvested by the Ojibwe.

fire. It was also rubbed with berries and other seasonings and eaten as jerky, or pemmican. Ducks, partridge, and other wild birds were harvested and prepared similarly to other meats.

All parts of the animals were used. Hides were used to make clothing and footwear as well as floor coverings, blankets, and coverings over lodges. Feathers adorned clothing and lined bedding. Even the bones of animals were used. They were ground into powder and mixed with dried meat and grease.

The *wii-gi-waam* (wigwam) was made from trees, plants, and hides.

DWELLINGS

The Ojibwe on Madeline Island lived in wigwams, lodges, bark houses, and the *tipi*. Wigwam *(wii-gi-waam)* is an Ojibwe word that has become part of the English language. They were round or rectangular structures made of poles or saplings (young trees) that were tied together with basswood *(wigub)* twine. The frame was covered with hides, rushes (a marsh plant), or the bark of black ash, birch, or elm. Hide blankets were hung over the door opening. The roof had a smoke hole for the fire, and the floors were covered with cedar boughs, rush mats, and hides.

The whole family helped build birch-bark canoes.

Peaked lodges were also used. These structures looked a lot like today's A-frame houses, with a long ridgepole across the center and poles down the sides. These homes were covered with the same materials as wigwams. Bark houses were used, especially in maple-sugar camps. These structures had straight walls and either domed or peaked roofs, much like today's houses. They were typically covered with the bark of birch, elm, or cedar. The tipi was also used. Spruce poles were put into a cone-shaped framework and covered with bark or hides.

THE HILLS OF LIFE

The Ojibwe living on Madeline Island followed an old teaching about life and its purpose. They viewed a person's life as a journey having four hills. Each hill has its own set of challenges and opportunities.

The first hill is from birth to infancy. Babies are born frail and dependent upon their parents. At first they are without much of a personality. They laugh and cry, and speak a language understood only by other babies. In a short span of time they learn to crawl, then walk, and

The first hill of life is from birth to infancy.

soon they are uttering words. In infancy they would be given names, one of the most important events in their lives. Names were given by respected elders at a feast held in honor of the child. It was the duty of parents to teach their children to live out the ideals (values or meanings) of the names the children were given.

The second hill is youth, a period from infancy to young adulthood. During this time young people learned the skills of living—hunting, gathering, and making things. They were also instructed in moral teachings. One of the most important of these teachings was to be kind to everyone. Elders did not really teach manners; they taught kindness in the way they themselves lived their lives. Listening to elders, helping those in need, feeding the hungry, visiting the lonely, and sharing whatever they had with others are examples of being kind.

Young people were also taught the importance of understanding their dreams, because dreams are a young person's first visions. A young man was not considered an adult until he had received his vision, which would give him his life purpose. When it was time for him to seek his vision, he would be brought to a small lodge (built by his father especially for that purpose) away from the village and left for three to four days. On Madeline Island, these places for seeking visions were probably on the more remote, eastern side of the island. Left without food during this time, a young man was told to think about his purpose in life and to seek his vision. Most young men would come away from these vision quests with a dream. With the help of an

elder who interpreted dreams, the quest would give them direction on how they should live their lives.

Young women also sought visions, but it was not a necessary part of their transition from youth to adulthood. The Ojibwe believe that all females are born knowing the purpose of life because young women have the ability to create life itself (have babies).

The second hill of life is youth, a period from infancy to young adulthood.

On Madeline Island, the places for seeking visions were probably on the more remote, eastern side.

women. There are battles to be fought; disputes to be resolved; and provisions to be obtained.... In form and scope and variety, the third hill is the most formidable of all.[19]

The fourth hill is being an elder. If elders have lived out their visions and followed the Good Path, they will have achieved wisdom. They will experience joy in the company of their grandchildren and nephews and nieces. They will be filled with stories about their own lives to serve as lessons to the young. Some will grow to be so old they will become like children again and need the care of adults to continue living. When elders reach the top of the fourth hill, they see all of their life spread out before them. As they begin their journey down the final hill, they will enter a mist. Here, their life on this Earth will end and they will enter the afterlife. And in the mist, they will make that final journey to a place of infinite beauty and plenty.

The third hill is adulthood:

In character the third hill is less steep and less rugged than the first two. It is not less difficult to climb. The burdens and duties of parenthood must be discharged. The weight and uncertainties of leadership must be borne by men and

The journey through life began and was completed by many Ojibwe generations on Madeline Island. Babies were born, youth sought their visions, adults raised families, and elders offered their wisdom. A burial ground in the village of LaPointe still marks the final resting place for some of the island's Ojibwe residents.

In the third hill of life, many men and women joined as partners.

In the third hill of life, the duties of adulthood must be fulfilled. Here, adults boil maple sugar.

THE COMING OF THE LIGHT-SKINNED RACE

The prophet of the Fourth Fire had told the people of the coming of the light-skinned race, and that prophecy would come true. An important medicine person (healer) who lived on Madeline Island, who was named *Ma-se-wa-pe-ga* (whole ribs), had a dream of light-skinned people who lived toward the rising sun. He decided he would go to find them. His fellow villagers discouraged him from going because the journey would be dangerous. In the area around the island were their enemies the Fox and Dakota. To the east were the Iroquois, the Ojibwe people's traditional enemies.

But the next spring, Ma-se-wa-pe-ga constructed a new birch-bark canoe, took provisions (food and clothing), and set out with his wife for the east. After a long journey back through the Great Lakes, he came along the shoreline and met white people. They welcomed him and his wife into their home. When it was time for him to return to Madeline Island, they gave him gifts of cloth, beads, and a steel knife and axe.

Ma-se-wa-pe-ga returned to his homeland with these

The fourth hill of life is being an elder.

from Michigan, Wisconsin, and much of Minnesota. With alcohol, they would nearly destroy themselves and their culture. The disease of alcoholism continues to ravage our people to the present day.

It would not be long before whites visited the Ojibwe people living on the island, and the Ojibwe world would be forever changed. A French explorer, Etienne Brule, visited them around 1620, about the same time the Pilgrims landed on Plymouth Rock. About 1660, two French explorers and traders, Medard Chouart Des Groseilliers and Pierre-Esprit Radisson, came to Madeline Island. Jesuit missionaries followed the traders, and soon a mission was established.

The Ojibwe welcomed the French as brothers and sisters and showed them kindness. The island's name was soon changed from Moningwanakaning to Madeline Island, renamed for an Ojibwe woman, Madeline Cadotte, who was the wife of trader Michael Cadotte. She was the daughter of White Crane. And, for the most part, the Ojibwe showed kindness to all the Europeans, and later the Americans, that were to follow, because the value of *being kind to everyone* was so deeply a part of our belief system.

gifts and the story of his travel. The next spring, a large party of Ojibwe went back east with beaver pelts to trade. They returned with firearms and alcohol. These two trade goods would forever change the way of life for the Ojibwe people. With superior weaponry, they would defeat their enemies, driving the Fox and Dakota

ACTIVITIES

TEST YOUR MEMORY

- Why did the Ojibwe eventually settle on Madeline Island?
  What was their life like on the island?
  What happened to the Ojibwe on the island?

- The Ojibwe living on Madeline Island lived according to the seasons. How did they live, even thrive, on the island?
  What seasonal activities were involved?

- What are the "four hills of life"?
  What does the story have to say about life and the meaning of life?

GOOD PATH PROJECTS

- Kindness is a trait admired throughout the world, among all people.
  What is kindness?
  What are examples of it?
  Why can it sometimes be so hard to be kind?
  Write a poem about kindness or someone you know who does kind acts.
  Draw a picture that illustrates an act of kindness.

- Use books and the computer to learn what Madeline Island is like today.

My ancestors were converted Catholics. They came from Madeline Island and settled in Red Cliff and Fond du Lac, places that eventually became part of Ojibwe country. As children we were marched off to Sunday mass. I became an altar boy. One of my grandmothers made me sit in the front row of the church— "where the sinners sit," she would say. We were told that all of us were born with mortal sin. But I have always believed there are many paths to the truth. The vestments I wore as an altar boy never fit me well. I was no angel. And as soon as I was old enough to make my own decisions, I went among our traditional people. Their prayers and songs made me feel whole. Their ways were buried in my ancestral memory. And along this path I am on.

—Thomas Peacock

BE MODERATE IN OUR THOUGHTS, WORDS, AND DEEDS

CHAPTER SEVEN

The Suffering of the Elder Brothers

Our Ojibwe ancestors often told stories to reinforce (strengthen) the values of the Good Path. This story reinforced the value of *being moderate in our thoughts, words, and deeds.*

An old Ojibwe tale tells of a time when all the herd animals disappeared. The meadows and forests were without the caribou, moose, and deer. Their well-worn paths were beginning to grow over. Without these animals, humankind was without much of its food supply because, in those times, animals offered themselves freely to humans as food.

The people searched the world for the animals but could not find them. Finally, an owl traveling in the far north came upon a herd so large it extended beyond the horizon. The animals seemed content. Just as it flew down to ask the animals why they had abandoned the

Ojibwe, the owl was attacked by a flock of crows. The owl barely escaped with its life.

Upon returning to the Ojibwe, the owl told them about what it had seen.

The tobacco pouch is used to help keep traditional spiritual values of the Ojibwe.

Upon returning to the Ojibwe, the owl told them about what it had seen. They quickly organized a war party and began their journey north to bring the herd animals back. Upon reaching the far north and seeing the herd, they were attacked by many thousands of crows. The battle went on for days and the animals just watched, seemingly not concerned. The Ojibwe were becoming discouraged, so their leader asked for a truce and an opportunity to meet with the animals. The crows agreed.

The leader of the deer explained to the Ojibwe that the reason they left was that they were being mistreated. "We had to leave," the leader said. "You were not respecting us. You did not eat all of our flesh. You left our bones lie carelessly about. You spoiled our forests." Only when the Ojibwe promised to honor and respect all life, including the animals, did the moose, deer, and caribou agree to return to the land of the Ojibwe. The moral of this tale would return to haunt the Ojibwe with the coming of Europeans and the fur trade.

THE OJIBWE LEAVE MADELINE ISLAND

If we estimate the beginning of the people's great westward migration at approximately A.D. 900, then the Ojibwe arrived on Madeline Island around the year 1400. For a span of three generations (120 to 150 years, by Ojibwe definition), they lived in relative peace on Madeline Island before they heard stories about the arrival of the light-skinned race from the Ojibwe who lived near Sault Sainte Marie:

One of the chiefs on Madeline Island kept a special o-za-wa-bik' (copper medallion) in his sacred Mide [Midewiwin, the Ojibwe medicine society] bundle. . . . His grandfathers had carved a notch on the edge of the medallion when the

Ojibway first settled on Madeline Island. . . . A new notch was carved on the medallion and it was carried again for another lifetime. In this way a record was kept of the generations of Ojibway that lived on Madeline Island. By the third notch carved on the copper disc was also inscribed the figure of a man wearing a large hat. It is believed that this represents the time in which the Ojibway of Madeline Island first heard of the arrival of the long-awaited Light-skinned race.[20]

It would be nearly one hundred years until the first French traders and explorers visited the island. Missionaries arrived soon after the first traders and began to convert the Ojibwe from their long-held spiritual beliefs to Christianity. The superior weaponry and tools of the Europeans probably made it easier to convince some Ojibwe that the Europeans had a superior god. Many of these early missionaries thought Ojibwe spiritual beliefs were demon worship, and they mistakenly referred to the traditional Ojibwe as pagans (people who don't believe in God).

In many ways, however, the beliefs of the Ojibwe and whites were similar. Both believed in one Creator, or God, and their stories of the creation were almost identical. Both had stories of a great flood. Both had beliefs about the end time, when the earth would be destroyed because of humankind's mistreatment of each other and the earth.

Missionaries arrived soon after the first traders.

But the differences were easy to recognize, and the missionaries highlighted these differences. The Ojibwe believe that all things have a soul-spirit. To the missionaries, only humans have a soul. Traditional Ojibwe do not have a belief in the existence of hell or the devil. A fundamental difference was that the Ojibwe believe all humans are born pure, with the values of the Good Path in their hearts. Many of the missionaries believed that humans were born with mortal sin. Also, the rituals (songs, chants, dances, prayers) of worship of the Ojibwe were very different from the missionaries' hymns, prayers, and services.

As some of the Ojibwe became Christianized, they began to hold the traditional Ojibwe with little regard. Family members turned against each other and neighbors

The trade of animal furs for European goods would dominate the Ojibwe way of life until the early 1800s.

turned against neighbors. False rumors began to spread that the "pagan" Indians were communicating with evil spirits and even engaging in cannibalism (eating human flesh).

Amid all the anger and fear and mistrust, many Ojibwe left Madeline Island. The first Ojibwe settlements off the island were in Wisconsin at Bad River, La Courte Oreilles, and Red Cliff. Bad River was founded by *Babomnigoniboy* (Spreading Eagle) of the Loon clan, who brought his family from Madeline Island. These were mostly families of converted Protestants. La Courte Oreilles was settled by three brothers of the Bear clan who left Madeline Island. Some of the first Ojibwe residents to settle Buffalo Bay (later renamed Red Cliff) were descendants of converted Catholics from Madeline Island, and many of them were Loon clan people. Other Ojibwe moved back to Sault Sainte Marie.

By the time Michael Cadotte established a fur trading post on the island in 1693, the island had been abandoned. Groves of saplings covered the clearings where the village and gardens once thrived. Well-trodden paths were overgrown with brush. Conquering tribal nations by encouraging division among tribal people has

always been one of the most effective ways to destroy tribal cultures. If our Ojibwe ancestors had only known that, maybe history would have played out differently.

At the beginning of the fur trade, the French wanted beaver pelts.

THE OJIBWE AND THE FUR TRADE

In 1659 the French fur traders Pierre-Esprit Radisson and Medard Chouart Des Groseilliers arrived on Madeline Island, and trading animal furs for European goods would dominate the Ojibwe way of life in the area until the early 1800s. Madeline Island served as an important fur trade post for nearly 150 years. The French controlled the fur trade until the end of the French and Indian War of 1763. The British controlled the trade until the end of the War of 1812. The Americans controlled the trade until the end of the fur trade in the 1840s.

Women prepared beaver hides.

The near annihilation (killing off) of fur-bearing animals seemed in direct conflict with two fundamental Ojibwe teachings: *Honor our elder brothers* and *be moderate in our thoughts, words, and deeds.* How was it our Ojibwe ancestors became partners in the slaughter of their elder brothers?

For countless centuries the Ojibwe had lived according to the seasons, in harmony with the plants and animals of the earth. The earth provided everything they needed—food, clothing, and shelter. Food they couldn't get directly from nature they grew in gardens. This way of living is called a subsistence economy (an economy driven by what one needs to survive).

With the coming of the Europeans and their trade goods, animal furs were used like money to purchase iron kettles, skillets, knives, guns, gunpowder, beads, cloth, and alcohol. The desire to have these goods overrode age-old beliefs about the ways animals should be treated and about living a life of *moderation.* A materialist economy (an economy driven by the desire for material possessions) became accepted in Ojibwe country.

Their clay kettles, pots, and dishes were exchanged for copper and brass utensils; their comparatively harmless bow and arrow, knives and spears of bones, were thrown aside, and in their place they procured the fire-arm, steel knife, and tomahawk of the whites.[21]

At the beginning of the fur trade, the French wanted beaver pelts. In Europe the pelts were made into hats, coats, and other clothing items. Eventually, other fur-bearing animals would be trapped, including the marten, mink, and fisher. Toward the end of the fur trade, even bear and moose hides were being traded. A large French fur post was established in Grand Portage, Minnesota, and another one on Madeline Island. Later, the American Fur Trade Company would build a fort in St. Louis Bay, near present-day Duluth, Minnesota. One trader's journal gives an idea of the value of beaver pelts (each number equals one pelt):

Trade goods	Hudson Bay Company
Guns (all sizes)	14
Blankets	7
Axes	1
Gun powder	1 per lb.
Shot [for rifles]	1 per 4 lbs.[22]

The Ojibwe soon depended on the fur trade for their survival. They thought they needed these trade goods, even though they had survived for many centuries without them. Traders offered easy credit, letting the Ojibwe charge large purchases from the trading posts. To pay their bills, they would have to bring in a large number of furs the following season. The traders controlled both the price of the furs and whom the Ojibwe sold the furs to.

With the coming of Europeans and their trade goods, animal furs were used like money to purchase iron kettles, skillets, knives, guns, gunpowder, beads, cloth, and alcohol.

Because the Ojibwe economy now revolved around the fur trade, even food items became trade goods. Fewer people made items of bark or clay. Fewer people made bows, arrows, stone knives, axes, or clothing from animal hides. A whole way of life died with the fur trade. And when the animals had all but disappeared, there was nothing left to trade. The people had forgotten to *honor the elder brothers*. By becoming a part of a material culture, they had also forgotten to *be moderate in thought, words, and deeds*.

Toward the end of the fur-trade era, even bear and moose hides were being traded.

THE OJIBWE MOVE INTO WISCONSIN, MICHIGAN, MINNESOTA, NORTH DAKOTA, AND MONTANA

The firearms acquired through trade gave the Ojibwe a great advantage over their enemies, the Fox and Dakota, who still relied on the bow and arrow as well as the spear. The Ojibwe quickly conquered their enemies, pushing the Fox into southern Wisconsin. What remained of the Fox people eventually joined with the Sauk. Many of their descendants now live in Tama, Iowa, on the Mesquakie Reservation. The Dakota were eventually pushed into southern Minnesota. Bands of northern Ojibwe also settled in North Dakota, where many of their descendants now live on the Turtle Mountain Reservation. In Montana, a group of Ojibwe and Cree eventually found a home on the Rocky Boy Reservation.

THE OJIBWE LOSE THEIR LAND

Once a mighty Ojibwe nation stretched across all of central Canada and from Michigan to Montana. That ended with the taking of our land by the Canadian and American governments.

The white settlers saw a great frontier in the west. It was land for settling down and starting a new life, land for farming, land for mining, and land for harvesting the timber. And the only way to get it was to take it away from tribal nations. Greed for land overshadowed the value of moderation. Warfare and disease led to the complete destruction (death) of some tribes.

As for those native people who survived, the government tried to remove them from their land. The first attempt was to move all native people west of the Mississippi River. This led to forced marches, including the infamous "Trail of Tears." On that march, thousands of Cherokee died while being forcibly removed from their homelands in the eastern United States. Later, the

The American Fur Trade Company post thrived in St. Louis Bay, near present-day Duluth, Minnesota.

settlers wanted the land west of the Mississippi River opened for settlement, and it was decided that large sections of land would be set aside just for the natives. These lands, called reservations, would keep native people completely separated from whites. Government agents would deal with them. In many respects, these reservations were run like prison camps.

The settlers wanted still more land, so the government opened up reservation lands to white settlement. The government told native people that it would give each native family enough land for a farm and allow them to own it. The natives were allowed to sell their land if they wished. To do so, they had to be declared "competent" (capable of doing things to show they were worthy of making their own decisions). Competent often meant our ancestors had to learn to speak English or had to sign an agreement giving up their claim to be a tribal person, or had to allow their children to be educated by the whites.

The lands given to individual natives were called "allotments." If reservation land was not given in allotments, it was sold to settlers. However, even most of the individual allotment lands were soon lost when native people sold their land to pay debts they owed to nonnative businesspeople. This explains why most reservations in the United States today contain only a small patchwork of tribally owned land. Nonnative people own most land within many reservations' boundaries. The Red Lake Reservation in Minnesota was the only Ojibwe reservation that refused to be part of the allotment. The Ojibwe still own all the land on that reservation.

Ojibwe treaty signers gather in Washington, D.C.

TREATIES

Most of the Ojibwe land was lost in treaties. In these formal agreements, the U. S. government purchased the land from our ancestors for a small amount of money and a promise of annual provisions (such as flour or tools).

The first of these treaties, signed in 1781, and the last, made in 1929, were both in Canada. All of the important land cession treaties with the United States were made in the forty-eight years between 1819 and 1866.[23]

The treaties between bands of the Ojibwe and the

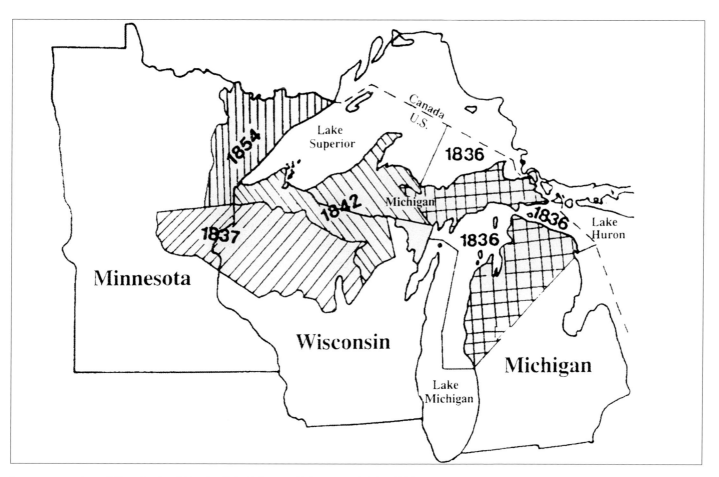

A treaty map shows Ojibwe lands within the United States, which were ceded by 1854.

United States are legal agreements between two nations. These agreements are still in effect to this day.

TREATY RIGHTS

In many of the treaties between the federal government and the Ojibwe people, the Ojibwe insisted on their right to continue to hunt, fish, and gather on the land they sold. The land they sold is often called "ceded" territory. They knew the small reservations they were being put on would not contain all the things, especially food, that they would need to live. Therefore, many of the treaties guarantee (promise) the Ojibwe the right to hunt, fish, and gather on the land they "ceded" to the federal government. Ojibwe people still hunt, fish, and gather on reservation-owned and ceded lands today.

A TROUBLED TIME

In the short period of time from their initial contact with Europeans, the Ojibwe had changed from a subsistence economy to a materialist economy. The desire for material possessions had overshadowed the value

The Ojibwe of Fond du Lac receive their last annuity payments (1865).

of *being moderate in thought, words, and deeds.* They had moved from their great homeland of Madeline Island to Wisconsin, Michigan, Minnesota, North Dakota, and Montana. But they quickly lost nearly all of the land to white settlers. Game was scarce in the forests where they hunted for food. Many Ojibwe were forced to rely on government rations (food allowances such as flour and salt pork) to avoid starvation. Malnutrition and starvation visited many Ojibwe villages.

A dark time was to follow, and it would last for a long time.

ACTIVITIES

- What does the Ojibwe story about the disappearance of the herd animals say about humankind's responsibility to care for the animals and plants of the earth?
  What are responsible ways to manage wildlife and other natural resources?

- What were the roles of the different people in the fur trade?
  The French?
  The Americans?
  The Ojibwe?

- The Ojibwe culture changed from a subsistence economy to an economy based on material possessions as a result of the fur trade. What does that mean?
  What kind of economy do we have today?

- How did the Ojibwe lose their land?

- Create your own trading economy with your friends with everyday materials available.
  What would things be worth in trade?
  Who would set the prices?
  What would be the impact of supply and demand?

- Make a map of Minnesota, Wisconsin, Michigan, North Dakota, and Montana, showing the locations of the different Ojibwe reservations as they exist today.

- Use books and the computer to learn about treaties that led to the establishment of Ojibwe reservations. Create a list of reservations and treaties.

One year we buried eight of my friends and relatives, including my sister. Most were lost through alcohol and cars slamming into trees. What lessons can we learn from their deaths? I know I have buried too many of my loved ones over the years. There are no lessons in that.

—Thomas Peacock

BE COURAGEOUS

CHAPTER EIGHT

The Time of the Sixth Fire

The prophet of the Fifth Fire told of a time when the Ojibwe people would be influenced by false promises. One false promise was that material possessions would lead to happiness and fulfillment. The other false promise was that forgetting the Ojibwe ways and adopting the ways of the white man would be for their betterment:

In the time of the Sixth Fire it will be evident that the promise of the Fifth Fire came in a false way. Those deceived by this promise will take their children away from the teachings of the chi'-ah-ya-og' (elders). Grandsons and granddaughters will turn against their elders. In this way the elders will lose their reason for living . . . they will lose their purpose in life. At this time a new sickness will come among the people. The balance of many people will be disturbed. The cup of life will almost be spilled. The cup of life will almost become the cup of grief.[24]

The prophet of the Sixth Fire had predicted a troubling time for Ojibwe people, and the prophet's words came true. To survive this time, the people would have to *be courageous.*

Many people suffered physically, emotionally, and spiritually. Diseases such as smallpox, influenza (flu), and tuberculosis swept through Ojibwe villages and claimed many lives. Native people had no immunity from these diseases, which the European settlers had brought to the Americas. There were also the diseases of diabetes, heart disease, and alcoholism. These diseases still kill many Ojibwe people. Poor nutrition, especially obesity (being overweight), became a problem. The Ojibwe were eating too many starchy foods (macaroni, bread, white rice) and no longer relied on wild game and garden produce as their main sources of food.

Our ancestors suffered emotionally as well. Families and communities were overcome with grief from losing too many loved ones, from losing their land, and from not having jobs or money to make ends meet. To further complicate their lives, racism (hatred of native people by non-Indians) was common in many communities that bordered reservations. A prolonged sadness, or grieving, fell over the Ojibwe people and continued from generation to generation. Many people suffered from broken spirits (broken hearts) as a result of losing relatives to alcoholism, poverty, and disease. It was as if the Ojibwe world had been turned upside down.

SUFFERING FROM WAR AND DISEASE

The first to suffer were our Lenape relatives who had stayed on the East Coast rather than migrate westward. Wars between the natives and English were brutal. The English used a tactic that the Spanish had used on the native people of Central and South America: kill everyone in villages, even women, children, and elders. The purpose of this type of warfare was to demoralize their enemy (make them want to give up). The Pequot tribe was nearly destroyed by disease and warfare with the Pilgrims. Disease and warfare reduced the Wampanoag tribe from more than three thousand to barely three hundred.

Our Dakota neighbors suffered greatly from warfare with the American government. Black Elk, an Oglala spiritual man, told of the infamous massacre in the South Dakota hamlet of Wounded Knee:

Dead and wounded women and children and little babies were scattered all along there where they had been trying to run away. The soldiers had followed along the gulch, as they ran, and murdered them in there. Sometimes they were in heaps because they had huddled together, and some were scattered all along.[25]

A group of Ojibwe people suffered a similar fate in 1850. They were told to go to Sandy Lake, near present-day McGregor, Minnesota, for their annuity payments (annual payments in cash and goods for the land they had sold the government in treaties). Three thousand native people went to Sandy Lake, but four hundred Ojibwe men, women, and children died when the food goods they were promised never arrived. Winter came.

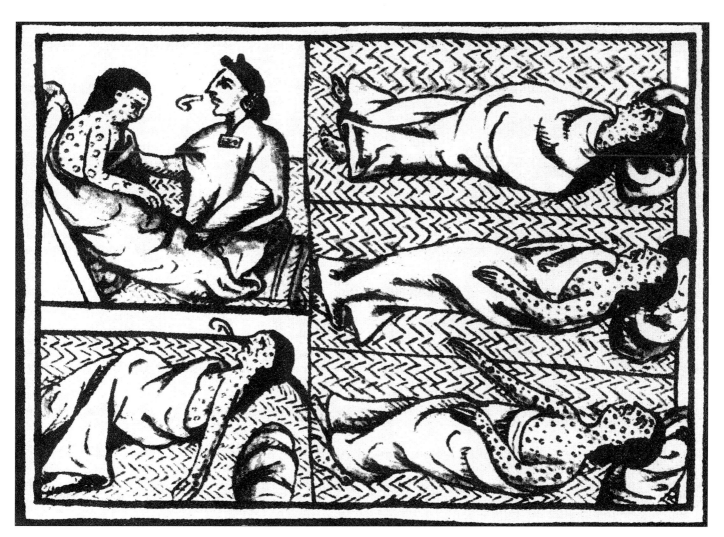

Diseases such as smallpox, influenza, and measles swept through Ojibwe villages and claimed many lives.

Ojibwe people were urged to build houses from lumber, which soon replaced the wigwam.

One hundred and seventy Ojibwe died of exposure, starvation, and disease at Sandy Lake and another 270 died on their way home.

THE FALSE PROMISE OF MATERIAL CULTURE

The Ojibwe became dependent on the fur trade for their livelihood and acquired a taste for owning things: the white man's clothing, firearms, alcohol, furniture, lumber, household goods (flour, molasses, spoons, forks, knives, kettles), and implements (horses, wagons). When the fur trade ended because there was no longer a demand for furs and because there were few animals to trap, the Ojibwe had no means to survive.

Food was scarce. Men had to travel far from their villages in search of game. The food gathered in making wild rice and gardening was not enough for the people to survive. Some men found work in the lumber camps that were springing up all over Ojibwe country. But for the most part the people were poor. The elderly and children suffered the most. There was malnutrition and starvation from not having enough healthful foods to eat.

When people are poor and desperate and see no way out, they lose hope. The loss of hope turns into despair. Some men began to drink to ease the pain they felt because they were no longer able to provide for their families. This was a bad time, and it would become even worse.

THE TAKING OF THE CHILDREN

Amid this despair, the federal government developed a plan to get native people to forget their tribal ways and adopt the ways of the white man. The idea was to take native children and put them in federal boarding and

Ojibwe children were taught to do farm work in many boarding schools.

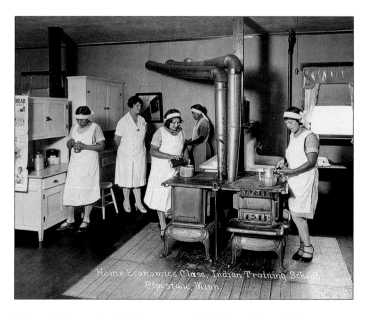

Ojibwe girls were taught home economics in boarding schools.

mission schools. Boarding and mission schools were built in Mount Pleasant, Michigan; Odana, Wisconsin; Tower, Pipestone, and White Earth, Minnesota; and Flandreau, South Dakota. These schools were operated by the federal government or by church organizations.

Ojibwe children were removed from their families during the school year. In the summer, many were sent to work on the farms of white settlers. Some didn't see their parents for years. At these schools, speaking the Ojibwe language was forbidden and punished by spankings, being put into isolation (removed from others), and losing privileges (like not being able to go to town on Saturdays). Young people were urged to report when other children violated this rule. They were also told that their Ojibwe ways were not worth knowing and that they should forget them and adopt the ways of the white man.

These schools had a lasting and devastating (awful) effect on Ojibwe people. Many young people who were raised in these schools eventually returned to their reservations. Because many had forgotten their Ojibwe language, they could no longer communicate with their elders. For many centuries, elders had been the primary teachers of the history, culture, and values of the Ojibwe people.

Many Ojibwe children were removed from their families during their boarding-school years.

At boarding schools, many Ojibwe young people were urged to forget their tribal ways and adopt the ways of the white man.

The young people had been told at school that their native ways were inferior to (not as good as) the ways of the white man. When these young people became adults, many of them did not teach the language or the Ojibwe ways to their children. Their own schooling had been much too painful. They had been punished for being Ojibwe. They did not want their children to suffer a similar fate.

During this same period, many Ojibwe children were also being removed from their homes and placed in non-native foster and adoptive homes. The ills that go along with poverty (families breaking up, alcoholism, and lack of jobs to support a family) led church and welfare agencies to take many of these children off the reservation.

Can you imagine having to give up your own children? Can you imagine the heartbreak parents felt in losing their children to boarding and mission schools?

THE BANNING OF OJIBWE SPIRITUAL PRACTICES

During this same time, federal law banned Ojibwe spiritual practices. Ojibwe people were urged to become

Three girls pose at boarding school, about 1900.

Mille Lacs Ojibwe young people leave for boarding school, about 1940.

Christians. Many, however, still practiced their traditional teachings. Ceremonies were still held in secret locations in many of our communities. Not until 1978, with the passing of the American Indian Religious Freedom Act, would native people again have religious freedom in this country.

Life was hard for many Ojibwe people during the time of the Sixth Fire.

THE LOSS OF HARMONY AND BALANCE

Ojibwe people have always believed that harmony and balance among the physical, emotional, and spiritual parts of our lives are needed to feel happy and fulfilled. First, we must attend to our physical needs—food, clothing, shelter, and physical health. Because of the extreme poverty in many Ojibwe communities, it was difficult to meet these needs.

Second, we must attend to our emotional needs—to love and to be loved, to have a sense of belonging, and to have feelings of self-worth. Because of boarding schools, the loss of Ojibwe ways, and the social ills (like alcoholism) that were common in our communities, it was difficult to meet these needs.

Third, we must attend to our spiritual needs—to worship the Creator freely and to live out *mino-bi-maadiziwin* (the Good Path) in our daily lives. Because Ojibwe spiritual beliefs were banned by law, and because of the deep despair in our communities, it was difficult to meet these needs.

The Ojibwe believe that if only one of these needs is

out of harmony, it will negatively affect the others. If we are physically ill, it can negatively affect our emotional well-being. If we are dealing with difficult emotional issues, it can affect us physically and spiritually. If we are angry and we carry anger inside of us for a long time, it can eventually make us physically ill. If we are sad and we feel sad for a long time, it will eventually make us physically ill. If our spiritual needs are not met, we will be affected emotionally and, possibly, physically.

During this dark time of our history, whole communities were out of harmony and balance. This has continued up to today. All the awful things we sometimes see in our communities—alcoholism, drug abuse, car accidents,

Ojibwe people were urged to become Christians.

gangs, sexual and physical abuse, poverty, crime, diabetes, heart disease, obesity, mental illness—all of those things come from being out of harmony and balance.

Our great-grandparents, grandparents, and parents lived during a difficult time. To survive and remain hopeful about the future, they had to be courageous. Deep in their hearts, they remained Ojibwe. Some would make sure the language survived. Others would make sure the beliefs and ways survived. Young Ojibwe people still live in communities that are experiencing problems similar to our ancestors.' They too need to *be courageous.*

THE HIDING OF THE
SACRED SCROLLS

During the time of great suffering, the spiritual people of the Ojibwe hoped that things would change for the better. When things didn't get better, they took the sacred teachings of the people, written on bark scrolls and passed down for countless generations, and hid them:

They gathered all the sacred bundles. They gathered all the Wee'-gwas [birch bark] scrolls that recorded the ceremo-

nies. All of these things were placed in a hollowed-out log from Ma-none' (the ironwood tree). They dug a hole in the cliff and buried the log where no one could find it.[26]

There is an old story among the Ojibwe that when the forest no longer senses the presence of Ojibwe people, the *si-si-gwad* (the sound trees make when their branches rub together) will make a sound of mourning. And the forest will weep.

And the forest wept.

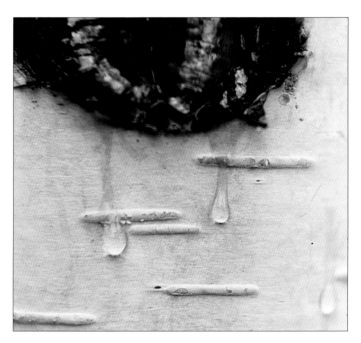

And the forest wept (weeping birch) . . .

ACTIVITIES

TEST YOUR MEMORY

- ◆ Why were Ojibwe children sent to boarding schools and mission schools?
  What was life like in these schools?
  What would you do if you were forced to go to a boarding school without your consent or against your parents' wishes?

GOOD PATH PROJECTS

- ◆ What is courage?
  What are some examples of courage?
  When have you shown courage?
  Interview someone you know who has shown great courage.

- ◆ Think about what it is like to be sick with the flu, a cold, or another form of illness.
  Use books and the computer to learn about the diseases that devastated many native communities (measles, smallpox, influenza).

- ◆ Diseases like smallpox were sometimes purposely introduced in trading blankets to native people, causing the death of entire villages, even entire tribes. This was an early form of biological warfare. Use books and the computer to learn about modern forms of biological warfare (like anthrax) and how we can prevent their use.

- ◆ Use books and the computer to learn about poverty.
  What is it like to be poor?
  What is it like having no voice to speak on your behalf in your community, county, state, or nation?

It is not my place to guess what the future will bring for my grandchildren or for their children. I can only pray that they will be happy living in the circle of love of their family. I hope they know and pass on the story of our people. It is a good story, one that began at the dawn of time and includes all of their relatives. Each generation has added its own story to it, and in that way the circle of the story grows. And in that way it goes on forever. Take my hand. Join in this most sacred of circles.

—Thomas Peacock

KEEP OUR PROMISES

CHAPTER NINE

The Seventh Generation

The forest wept for many generations. But if the prophecy of the Seventh Fire comes true, the bad times will end soon. Things will get better. If we listen carefully, we might hear a changing in the winds.

How do the Ojibwe know this? We already see among us *osh-ki-bi-ma-di-zeeg'* (new people). The new people listen to the elders who still know the old ways and they are learning from them. Who are the new people? They are the ones singing, dancing, and attending our powwows. They are learning our language. They are bringing food plates to elders at our gatherings. And they are slowly managing to walk away from the drugs and gangs and despair and all the sickness that has visited our villages for these many generations. They will relight the sacred fire, and its warmth and light will reach even the most remote (farthest away) of our villages. The new people are living out the value of *keeping our promises*, both to our ancestors and to generations to come, by ensuring that Ojibwe ways (language, culture, and values) continue into the future.

Passing down the story of our people ensures our future.

THE OJIBWE LANGUAGE

When our ancestors were taken away to boarding and mission schools, the language was almost lost. Children who returned from these schools and still knew how to speak Ojibwe usually didn't teach it to their children. The English language quickly replaced Ojibwe as the everyday language spoken in homes.

English was the language of the church, government, and daily life. With the coming of radio and television, the English language became the main language for entertainment and news. Ojibwe was still spoken in ceremonies and among the elderly, but it was viewed as a dying language. As each elder passed on to the spirit world, the numbers of speakers dwindled. In some communities, all one could hear was English. We were fortunate to have had a few people in each community who taught the language to their children so the language can still be heard today.

Parts of the language survived in daily use, including *aaniin* (hello) and *niijii* (friend). Some of the language even became part of the English language, including *makizin* (moccasin) and *mooz* (moose). Some cities and towns have Ojibwe names, including *Ogema* (leader), *Odana* (town), and *Bena* (benay, bird). And many Ojibwe children still learn basic words, like numbers and animals, from parents and grandparents: *bezhig* (one), *niizh* (two), *niswa* (three), *niiwin* (four), and *naanan* (five); and *makwa* (bear), *migizi* (eagle), and *ma'iingan* (wolf). But the true essence (meaning) of who we are is in the language. Our culture (everything that makes us Ojibwe) is in our language.

Since the arrival of the new people, relearning the language has become an important goal of many Ojibwe

Everywhere in Ojibwe country we see people in Ojibwe-language classes.

people. Elders and others who speak the language are teaching the language. There are, however, some people who say it doesn't matter or isn't important. They ask, "If you learn the language, whom will you speak it to when you go home? No one there speaks it." They ask, "What good is the language? You can't use it on the job or out in the world. You should concentrate on learning one of the world languages, like Russian, Spanish, or Japanese. Ojibwe language is the past. You need to concentrate on the future."

The new people and their elder teachers, however, know that before we can become part of the larger world, we need to first know *who we are.* One way to do that is to learn our language. And unlike the world languages, there is nowhere else in the world where Ojibwe is spoken or written. So everywhere in Ojibwe country we see people in Ojibwe-language classes. Language societies, groups of everyday people interested in learning the language, are appearing in many of our communities. Language-immersion camps and schools (where only Ojibwe is spoken) are forming. We are seeing more and more people who speak the language.

Aaniin ezhi ayaa yan? (How are you doing?)

Nimino, aya. Giindush? (I'm fine. And you?)

The new people will learn the language. They will teach it to their children. And, in turn, their children will teach it to their children. That is our future.

OJIBWE CULTURE

What is culture? Culture is the shared beliefs, values, music, art, and ways of a group of people. Along with the rebirth of the language there has been a growing interest in Ojibwe culture. Powwows, namings (where young people are given Ojibwe names by elders and

Parents pass Ojibwe culture on to their children.

other traditional people), and ceremonies are becoming more common in Ojibwe country.

Ojibwe people are beginning to celebrate their successes. In some schools, young Ojibwe people are given special feasts and awards for doing well in school. More Ojibwe are recognizing the acquired wisdom of elders and traditional people when they give them gifts of tobacco *(asema),* blankets, and sage. Slowly, people are beginning to listen well, think before they speak, and speak only when they have something important to say. They are learning to recognize all forms of leadership as important, including political leaders (who must conduct our dealings with the outside world), spiritual leaders, and everyday community leaders (who work with children, the sick, and the elderly). All of these things are old Ojibwe ways (parts of the culture) that are becoming common in our communities again.

At the same time, the Ojibwe are Americans and part of American culture. Like all Americans, we go to concerts and sporting events. Many of us love fast food, shopping malls, and movie theaters just like everyone else. Through schooling and the mass media (radio, television, and the Internet), we learn all about American culture. We speak English, want all the latest fashions, and worry about our jobs and the future as do most people.

Being Ojibwe doesn't mean we have to choose between being an American or an Ojibwe. We can be Ojibwe and be Americans. After all, native people were the first citizens of this land. Ojibwe warriors have fought in America's wars to protect our rights of freedom. Knowing who we are as Ojibwe people will actually make us even better American citizens.

THE GOOD PATH

Generations of Ojibwe people lost their way along the Good Path. Life was hard, and some could not deal with the difficulties. Poverty and all of the things that sometimes go along with being poor led to alcoholism, drugs, violence, and a lack of hope in many of our communities. Then things began to change. Just as there was a renewed interest in the Ojibwe language and culture, more and more people began following the Good Path, the values they were given by the Creator at birth.

According to Ojibwe beliefs, the Creator gave each

human a special gift at the time of his or her birth. Each and every one of us was given some of the Mystery, some of the Creator. The parts of each of us that come directly from the Creator are the values of the Good Path. Each of us was born with these values already in our hearts. Ojibwe people also believe that the only way individuals can find the Good Path is by looking inside their own hearts.

And the journey back onto the Good Path, to a life free from alcohol, drugs, violence, and lack of hope, has been led by the new people and their elder teachers. They said, "Maybe we have had the solutions to our problems all along. Maybe the answers are inside us. We should look deep inside ourselves. There we will find the answers." Megan, an Ojibwe student, said:

She [my cousin] told me never to turn out like she did—to stay in school and always do really well. And to never let drugs or alcohol stop me. And I've had plenty of chances and plenty of temptations, and I may have been sidetracked, but I never let them stop me. You have to be a pure person, and you have to respect yourself and others, and that has definitely influenced me. Like all the elders that have taught me along that road.[27]

Ojibwe veterans are honored for protecting the country's rights of freedom.

Ojibwe people have assumed their important role in protecting the environment.

Families engage in the moose harvest.

Healing ourselves and our communities will take a long time. Just as our communities have been ill for many generations, it will probably take many more generations to become well again. But everywhere there are signs of hope. Most community gatherings in Ojibwe country are opened by a prayer to the Creator *(honor the Creator)*. Elder councils have formed to advise the people on important decisions and other matters *(honor elders)*. Communities are launching efforts to deal with the difficult issues of domestic abuse *(honor women)*. Ojibwe people have taken an important role in protecting the environment, and many of our communities have established natural resources and fish and wildlife departments *(honor our elder brothers)*. People are beginning to speak out against violence *(be peaceful)* in our villages, and violent people are being told they are no longer welcome. Ojibwe people are celebrating their successes as never before, by having honor banquets for successful students and by giving back to the community *(be kind)* through such volunteer work as tutoring, picking up litter along roadways and in housing projects, and visiting elders and the ill. There are now treatment centers for drugs and alcohol, programs for teen-pregnancy prevention, and programs for alcohol and drug prevention and intervention. Community health fairs are held in some communities to deal with obesity, alcohol and drug use, diabetes, heart disease, and the need for exercise *(be moderate)*.

The work that is being done to help Ojibwe people live better lives is being led by good people of all colors, races, and ages, and both genders. It is slow and difficult work. Good work is never easy. And it will take the efforts of many more courageous people *(be courageous)* until the work is complete. Patience is the key. Like people everywhere, the Ojibwe want a better life for themselves and their children. We are grateful to our ancestors. They survived a horrible period of history so the Ojibwe could be here today, still strong in our ways. And we acknowledge our responsibility to pass down the story of our people to future generations. We owe them that *(keep our promises)*.

The Good Path is celebrated at a Mash-ka-wisen sobriety powwow.

FULL CIRCLE

We dream of better times and a better life for ourselves and all who are important to us. And we live to make it real.

In the beginning, the Creator had a vision. And the Creator brought forth the vision by creating the universe with all of the galaxies, stars, planets, and moons. The Creator then made our beautiful Earth and filled it with oceans, lakes, rivers, and streams. The Creator then made all the kinds of plants and animals of the earth. Finally, the Creator made humankind in all shapes, sizes, colors, languages, and ways of living.

And the Creator gave humans the ability to have visions, to find their purpose or reasons for being here, knowing all along that people sometimes lose their way. Humans are imperfect beings. We all stray from the Good Path. Then we dream of better times and of a better life, for ourselves and for all who are important to us.

And we live to make it real.

That is what makes us human.

Maskawisen (Be strong). *Mi-iw* (That is all).

ACTIVITIES

TEST YOUR MEMORY

♦ What was the prophecy of the Seventh Fire?
How might the prophecy be coming true in Ojibwe communities?

♦ What are some traditional activities that are being practiced again in many
Ojibwe communities?
Why are these important?

♦ Who is responsible for ensuring that the Ojibwe people, culture, and philosophy live on
into the future?
How can this be done?

GOOD PATH PROJECTS

♦ List your some of your dreams about your future, or the future of our country or the world.
What can you do to make these dreams real?
What needs to happen to make these dreams come true?

♦ List the things you think could improve the world (world peace, the end of hunger, or saving the
environment, for example).
Help improve your own community by collecting food for a food shelf or raising money for
children in great poverty, such as in Afghanistan.

♦ Write a poem or short story or create a picture that illustrates one of the values of the Good Path.

♦ What is a promise? List the kinds of promises that are easy.
What kinds are difficult? What kinds of promises might we make for the people of the future
(our children and grandchildren)?

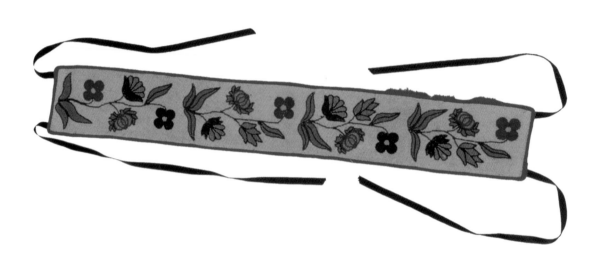

NOTES

CHAPTER ONE

1. Johnston, Basil. *Ojibway Heritage.* Lincoln: University of Nebraska Press, 1976, p. 12.
2. Benton-Banai, Eddie. *The Mishomis Book.* Hayward, Wisconsin: Indian Country Communications, 1988, p. 31.

CHAPTER TWO

3. McCutchen, David. *The Red Record: The Wallam Olum.* Garden City Park, New York: Avery Publishing Group, 1993, p. x.
4. McCutchen, *The Red Record,* p. 68.
5. McCutchen, *The Red Record,* p. 98.
6. McCutchen, *The Red Record,* p. 138.

CHAPTER THREE

7. Johnston, Basil. *Ojibway Heritage.* Lincoln: University of Nebraska Press, 1976, p. 17.
8. Broker, Ignatia. *Night Flying Woman.* St. Paul: Minnesota Historical Society Press, 1983, p. 33.

CHAPTER FOUR

9. Johnston, Basil. *Ojibway Heritage.* Lincoln: University of Nebraska Press, 1976, p. 33.
10. Benton-Banai, Eddie. *The Mishomis Book.* Hayward, Wisconsin: Indian Country Communications, 1988, p. 74.
11. Benton-Banai, *The Mishomis Book,* p. 89.
12. Benton-Banai, *The Mishomis Book,* p. 90.
13. Benton-Banai, *The Mishomis Book,* p. 91.
14. Benton-Banai, *The Mishomis Book,* p. 93.

CHAPTER FIVE

15. Warren, William. *History of the Ojibway Nation.* St. Paul: Minnesota Historical Society Press, 1984, p. 83.

CHAPTER SIX

16. Vizenor, Gerald. *The People Named the Chippewa.* Minneapolis: University of Minnesota Press, 1984, p. 47.
17. Warren, William. *History of the Ojibway Nation.* St. Paul: Minnesota Historical Society Press, 1984, p. 99.
18. Broker, Ignatia. *Night Flying Woman.* St. Paul: Minnesota Historical Society Press, 1983, p. 57.
19. Johnston, Basil. *Ojibway Heritage.* Lincoln: University of Nebraska Press, 1976, p. 115.

CHAPTER SEVEN

20. Benton-Banai, Eddie. *The Mishomis Book.* Hayward, Wisconsin: Indian Country Communications, 1988, p. 103.
21. Warren, William. *History of the Ojibway Nation.* St. Paul: Minnesota Historical Society Press, 1984, p. 126.
22. Ray, Arthur. *Indians in the Fur Trade.* Toronto: University of Toronto Press, 1974, p. 145.
23. Ojibwe Curriculum Committee. *The Land of the Ojibwe.* St. Paul: Minnesota Historical Society Press, 1973, p. 23.

CHAPTER EIGHT

24. Benton-Banai, Eddie. *The Mishomis Book.* Hayward, Wisconsin: Indian Country Communications, 1988, p. 90.
25. Neihardt, John. *Black Elk Speaks.* Lincoln: University of Nebraska Press, 1979, p. 259.
26. Benton-Banai, *The Mishomis Book,* p. 91.

CHAPTER NINE

27. Bergstrom, Amy, Miller-Cleary, Linda, and Peacock, Thomas. *The Seventh Generation: Native Youth Speak about Finding the Good Path.* Charleston, West Virginia: ERIC/CRESS, 2002.

BIBLIOGRAPHY

Benton-Banai, Eddie. *The Mishomis Book.* Hayward, Wisconsin: Indian Country Communications, 1988.

Bergstrom, Amy, Miller-Cleary, Linda, and Peacock, Thomas. *The Seventh Generation: Native Youth Speak about Finding the Good Path.* Charleston, West Virginia: ERIC/CRESS, 2002.

Broker, Ignatia. *Night Flying Woman.* St. Paul: Minnesota Historical Society Press, 1983.

Copway, George. "The Traditional History and Characteristic Sketches of the Ojibway Nation." In *Touchwood,* edited by Gerald Vizenor. St. Paul, Minnesota: New Rivers Press, 1987.

Densmore, Frances. *Chippewa Customs.* St. Paul: Minnesota Historical Society Press, 1979.

Johnston, Basil. *Ojibway Heritage.* Lincoln: University of Nebraska Press, 1976.

Johnston, Basil. *Ojibway Ceremonies.* Lincoln: University of Nebraska Press, 1982.

McCutchen, David. *The Red Record: The Wallam Olum.* Garden City Park, New York: Avery Publishing Group, 1993.

Neihardt, John. *Black Elk Speaks.* Lincoln: University of Nebraska Press, 1979.

Nichols, John, and Nyholm, Earl. *A Concise Dictionary of the Minnesota Ojibwe.* Minneapolis: University of Minnesota Press, 1995.

Ojibwe Curriculum Committee. *The Land of the Ojibwe.* St. Paul: Minnesota Historical Society Press, 1973.

Peacock, Thomas D., ed. *A Forever Story: The People and Community of the Fond du Lac Reservation.* Cloquet, Minnesota: Fond du Lac Band of Lake Superior Chippewa, 1988.

Peacock, Thomas, and Wisuri, Marlene. *Ojibwe: Waasa Inaabidaa (We Look in All Directions).* Afton, Minnesota: Afton Historical Society Press, 2002.

Ray, Arthur. *Indians in the Fur Trade.* Toronto: University of Toronto Press, 1974.

Vizenor, Gerald. *The People Named the Chippewa.* Minneapolis: University of Minnesota Press, 1984.

Warren, William. *History of the Ojibway Nation.* St. Paul: Minnesota Historical Society Press, 1984.

www.madelineisland.com/history.html

www.shsw.wisc.edu/sites/madisle/furtrade.html

ABOUT THE AUTHOR

Thomas Peacock, a member of the Fond du Lac Band of Lake Superior Chippewa, is an associate professor of education at the University of Minnesota–Duluth, where he teaches educational leadership. He completed both his master's and doctoral degrees at Harvard University. His earlier book for Afton Historical Society Press, *Ojibwe: Waasa Inaabidaa (We Look in All Directions)* is the companion book to a six-part public television documentary produced by WDSE-TV in Duluth.

ABOUT THE PHOTOGRAPHER

Marlene Wisuri's photographs have been exhibited regionally and nationally in numerous one-person and group exhibitions, as well as in Finland and Norway. She has a master's of fine arts degree from the University of Massachusetts–Dartmouth and taught photography and photographic history for more than twenty years at several colleges and universities. She has served as photographer or photo editor for a number of previous books. She is currently the director of the Carlton County Historical Society in Cloquet, Minnesota.

ACKNOWLEDGMENTS

We are grateful to many people who shared their talent and time to aid in the production of *The Good Path.*

We would like to thank our personal editors, Liz Bass, Valerie Tanner, and Elizabeth Albert-Peacock, who read early drafts of the manuscript and made significant and worthwhile changes.

Many thanks go to Carl Gawboy for so generously allowing us to use his beautiful artwork.

We would also like to thank photographers, curators, and collectors Monroe Killy, Rocky Wilkinson, Mike LeGarde, Linda Mayotte, Amoose, Jeff Amble, Tom Amble, Wendy Savage, Richard E. Nelson, Peter Spooner, and the Tweed Museum of Art, the Great Lakes Indian Fish and Wildlife Commission, the George W. Brown Jr. Ojibwe Museum and Cultural Center at Lac du Flambeau, Tom Urbanski at Fond du Lac Tribal and Community College, John Kahionhes Fadden, and others who helped along the way.

The enthusiastic support of Patricia Johnston, Chuck Johnston, Mary Susan Oleson, Michele Hodgson, and the staff at Afton Historical Society Press has been much appreciated.

And many thanks to our families for their support and patience.

ILLUSTRATION CREDITS

2. Ceremonial staff, photo by Kathy Olson
3. Ojibwe dolls, the Richard E. and Dorothy Rawlings Nelson Collection of American Indian Art, photo courtesy of Tweed Museum, University of Minnesota—Duluth
14. Galaxy, photo by D. Wang, CXC, NASA
15. Waves crashing, photo by Marlene Wisuri
16. Flower with bee, photo by Marlene Wisuri
17. Deer, photo courtesy of the Great Lakes Indian Fish and Wildlife Commission
18. *Humans Marveling,* drawing by John Kahionhes Fadden
19. *The Mourning Spirit,* pencil drawing by Frank Bigbear, the Richard E. and Dorothy Rawlings Nelson Collection of American Indian Art, photo courtesy of Tweed Museum, University of Minnesota—Duluth
20. Loon under water, photo by Larry Mishkar, Cornell Laboratory of Ornithology
22. Madeline Island, photo by Marlene Wisuri
26. *Storyteller,* acrylic on wood by Carl Gawboy
27. Wampum shells, photo by Marlene Wisuri
28. Pictograph, photo by Monroe Killy, Minnesota Historical Society
30. Ice fields, photo by Marlene Wisuri
32. Bison, *Scenes from Every Land,* ed. Gilbert H. Grosvenor, National Geographic Society, 1918
33. Delaware River, Detroit Publishing Co., Library of Congress
38. Moon, photo by Marlene Wisuri
39. Spirit tree, photo by Monroe Killy, Minnesota Historical Society
40. *Joining the Women,* watercolor by Carl Gawboy
41. *Basket Maker,* watercolor (or tempera) by Patrick Desjarlait, the Richard E. and Dorothy Rawlings Nelson Collection of American Indian Art, photo courtesy of Tweed Museum, University of Minnesota—Duluth
42. Woman and baby, Minnesota Historical Society
43. Mrs. Waboose, Minnesota Historical Society
43. Woman parching rice, photo by Monroe Killy, Minnesota Historical Society
44. *Watch on the Point,* watercolor by Carl Gawboy
45. Berry pickers, Milwaukee Public Museum
46. Winona LaDuke, photo by Keri Pickett
46. Grandmother and child, Bayliss Public Library
50. Tobacco, photo by Marlene Wisuri
51. Sweetgrass, photo by Marlene Wisuri
52. Clan symbols, *The Aborigines of Minnesota,* Minnesota Historical Society, 1911
53. Crane, photo by Robert Barber, Cornell Laboratory of Ornithology
54. *Bear,* watercolor by Robert L. KakayGeesic, collection of Min-no-aya-win Clinic
55. Wild rice and rainbow, photo by Marlene Wisuri
56. Megis shell, photo by Marlene Wisuri
57. Crafts using plants, aprons, the Richard E. and Dorothy Rawlings Nelson Collection of American Indian Art, photo courtesy of Tweed Museum, University of Minnesota—Duluth
57. Crafts using animals, quill box, the Richard E. and Dorothy Rawlings Nelson Collection of American Indian Art, photo courtesy of Tweed Museum, University of Minnesota—Duluth
58. Child, photo courtesy of the Great Lakes Indian Fish and Wild Life Commission
62. Lake Superior, photo by Marlene Wisuri
63. Ojibwe engraving, Fanny Corbaux, Minnesota Historical Society
64. Migration map, adapted from *The Land of the Ojibwe,* Minnesota Historical Society, 1973, and Tim Roufs
65. *Camp Site on the St. Lawrence,* Currier & Ives, Library of Congress
67. *Niagara Falls,* Thomas Davies, New-York Historical Society
68. *Michilimackinac,* from Castlenau, *Vues et Souvenir du Nord,* pl. 26, The Newberry Library
69. Fishing at Sault Ste. Marie, Detroit Publishing Co., Library of Congress
70. Spirit Island, photo by Marlene Wisuri

74. *La Pointe,* sketch by Aindi-bi-tunk, State Historical Society of Wisconsin, Whi (x3) 25367
75. Sunrise, photo by Marlene Wisuri
76. Boy ricing, photo by Monroe Killy, Minnesota Historical Society
77. *Woman Picking Berries,* by Carl Gawboy
78. *Winter Fishing,* watercolor by Carl Gawboy, collection of Min-no-aya-win Clinic
79. Wigwam, Carlton County Historical Society
79. Canoe-building, photo by T. W. Ingersoll, Minnesota Historical Society
80. Baby in cradleboard, photo by Carl Gustaf Linde, Minnesota Historical Society
81. Girl with baby, Minnesota Historical Society
82. Vision quest, photo by Marlene Wisuri
83. Wedding, photo by Benjamin Franklin Upton, Minnesota Historical Society
83. Middle age, photo by Monroe Killy, Minnesota Historical Society
84. Elder man, Minnesota Historical Society
87. Snowy owl, photo by Jeffrey Rich, Cornell Laboratory of Ornithology
88. Tobacco pouch, the Richard E. and Dorothy Rawlings Nelson Collection of American Indian Art, photo courtesy of Tweed Museum, University of Minnesota—Duluth
89. Missionary arrival, photo by Marlene Wisuri
90. Fur trading, photo by Marlene Wisuri
91. *Beaver,* painting by Noel DuCharme, collection of Wendy Savage
92. *Women Preparing Hides,* watercolor by Carl Gawboy
93. *Fur Trade,* drawing by W. A. Rogers for *Harper's Monthly Magazine,* June 1879, Minnesota Historical Society
94. Moose hide, photo by Monroe Killy, Minnesota Historical Society
95. *Fond du Lac Fur Post,* watercolor by Carl Gawboy
96. Treaty group in Washington, Brady's Galleries, Minnesota Historical Society
97. Treaty map, photo courtesy of Great Lakes Indian Fish and Wild Life Commission
98. Allotment payments, Minnesota Historical Society
101. Trees, photo by Marlene Wisuri
103. *Small Pox,* engraving by Fray Bernardinode Sahagun, *General History of the Things of New Spain*
104. Log house, collection of Jeff Amble
105. Boys working in field, Minnesota Historical Society
105. Girls' home-economics class, photo by C. E. Sogn, collection of Tom Amble
106. Boarding-school boys, George W. Brown Jr., Ojibwe Museum and Cultural Center, Lac du Flambeau
106. Boarding-school girls, George W. Brown Jr., Ojibwe Museum and Cultural Center, Lac du Flambeau
107. Girls at boarding school, George W. Brown, Jr., Ojibwe Museum and Cultural Center, Minnesota Historical Society
107. Pipestone school bus, photo by Zula Corning, Minnesota Historical Society
108. Hard times, photo by Frances Densmore, Minnesota Historical Society
109. Sunday school, photo by Smith and Wilkins, Minnesota Historical Society
110. Weeping birch, photo by Marlene Wisuri
113. Boy reading, photo by Rocky Wilkinson, Fond du Lac
114. Language class, photo by Kathy Strauss, *Duluth News Tribune*
115. Children learning ricing, photo by Amoose, *News From the Sloughs,* Bad River Band of Lake Superior Chippewa Indians
117. Veterans, photo by Amoose, *News from the Sloughs,* Bad River Band of Lake Superior Chippewa Indians
118. Migration journey, photo by Marlene Wisuri
118. Moose hunt, photo by Marlene Wisuri
119. Mash-ka-wisen sobriety powwow, photo by Marlene Wisuri
120. New dawn, photo by Marlene Wisuri
122. Ojibwe sash, the Richard E. and Dorothy Rawlings Nelson Collection of American Indian Art, photo courtesy of Tweed Museum, University of Minnesota—Duluth

This book was designed by

MARY SUSAN OLESON

Afton, Minnesota, &
Nashville, Tennessee

Fonts used:
Gill Sans and Benevento